T0163091

The Juice

THE JUICE

The Real Story of Baseball's Drug Problems

WILL CARROLL

WITH WILLIAM L. CARROLL, ED.D.

Foreword by Alan Schwarz

Ivan R. Dee

CHICAGO

www.ivanrdee.com

The paperback edition of this book carries the ISBN 1-56663-720-1.

Library of Congress Cataloging-in-Publication Data
Carroll, Will, 1970–
   The juice : the real story of baseball's drug problems / Will Carroll with William L. Carroll ; foreword by Alan Schwarz.
      p. cm.
   Includes index.
   ISBN 1-56663-668-X (hardcover : alk. paper)
   1. Doping in sports. 2. Athletes—Drug use. 3. Basketball players—Drug use.
   I. Carroll, William L. II. Title.
   RC1230.C37 2005
   362.29—dc22
                              2005007537

For Dick and Mary, and for all my teachers—W. C.

For my mother, and the University of Mobile—W. L. C.

Contents

Foreword by Alan Schwarz

Senior Writer, *Baseball America*

AS IF WE NEEDED further proof, the current rancor over steroids in baseball demonstrates yet again that talking about something, and talking about it intelligently, are two altogether different things. This past winter, as alleged testimony from the BALCO scandal was leaked to a panting press and Jose Canseco's book detonated like a nail bomb, you couldn't watch "SportsCenter" or listen to sports radio without most everyone sermonizing about steroids—despite having little, if any, concrete knowledge about the issues involved. Alas, the anarchic court of public opinion is far better at delivering verdicts than asking questions.

What are steroids in the first place, and how do they differ from legal supplements? Do these substances in fact aid baseball performance, and if so, how? What are their side effects, and how can those be detected? These and so many other issues became mere inconveniences to media just itching to draw conclusions from body types, statistics, and gossip. Steroids are Bad, the players should be Tested, and those caught should be Banned.

Now, the outrage is more than reasonable: players' use of illegal performance-enhancing drugs, whichever ones and to whatever degree, are a nefarious betrayal of the assumption of fair play at the heart of all games and records. But make no mistake, the intellectual sloppiness rampant in most steroid screeds—from columnists who haven't done their homework to radio yahoos airily accusing specific players—is in many ways far more dangerous than the steroids themselves.

It's in this realm that the book you're holding shines, and makes it one of the more important baseball volumes in recent memory. Will Carroll is not a conventional baseball journalist. He covers only the medical side of the game, a beat that has carved him out a unique place among today's writers. He talks to team trainers. He researches the extent and effects of injuries. And he isn't some crackpot working on the fringe: his writings for Baseball Prospectus are read not just by BP's ten thousand customers but by a surprising number of team personnel who use it as a valuable information source. When you hear that a general manager scuttled a trade after Will Carroll informed him of an unreported injury to one of the players involved, you realize how relevant his work has become.

What Will brings to the steroids issue is calm, measured analysis of a subject that too often drowns in sanctimonious pap. Rather than react, he thinks. Rather than guess, he inquires. He deconstructs the subject and builds it back with fact, from the bottom up. (Let's face it: of the thousands of people you hear pontificating on steroids, how many really, truly, know what they're talking about?) In this book you'll learn what a steroid is, and what its effects are. You'll learn how steroids differ from other performance-enhancing drugs and supplements, both against the rules of baseball and not. And there is far more than medical reporting: you'll not only meet a minor leaguer who paid off his drug tester with a $100 bill, but a teenager who injects himself right in front of Will, with his parents' permission and even encouragement.

The Juice is fueled not by the narcissism of Jose Canseco, the pro-scandal bent of the conventional press, or the agendas of Major League Baseball and the Players Association. It relies on pure inquisitiveness and the pursuit of reliable and useful truth. In this era of feigned strength, little can be more powerful.

The Juice

Introduction

I DIDN'T WANT to write this book.

My pal Tim Marchman, my contact at Ivan R. Dee, first broached the topic to me early in 2004, and I resisted. In the end, my objections led me to the point of putting pen to paper—or, in my case, fingers to keyboard. I interviewed Alan Schwarz while he was promoting his great book *The Numbers Game*, and a phrase from that interview echoed in my mind.

"I wrote the book," he said, "because I wanted to read it. It would have been much easier for me to have gone to the bookstore and bought it, but it wasn't there." Like his history of statistics, the material that follows is something I could not find, yet wanted to see in print.

The tipping point for me was the late 2004 revelations from leaked grand jury testimony regarding the BALCO (Bay Area Laboratory Cooperative) case. (I'll consistently refer to this legal case, named *United States v. Victor Conte et al.*, as the BALCO case for simplicity's sake.) Once it came to light that, willingly or unwillingly, knowingly or unknowingly, two of baseball's biggest names, Barry Bonds and Jason Giambi, were linked to the arena of performance-enhancing drugs, I waited and watched. Instead of seeing fact, I saw grandstanding. Instead of seeing science, I saw emotion. Instead of educating, the media merely incited.

It took me a couple of weeks to put together a feature piece—originally published at Baseball Prospectus—that forms the heart of this book. Built on research I had started while deciding whether or not to write this book, that piece elicited a greater response than almost anything I had ever written. To me it was simply a piece of research like any other: I found facts, spoke to experts, and tried to put the information together in a reasoned, evenhanded essay.

Some readers exploded because they felt I'd gone too far— but few agreed in which direction I'd gone too far. Many argued that I'd given up too much, siding with the commissioner of baseball and leaving the privacy rights of the players behind. Many felt that I should have called for the public hanging of anyone associated with or even suspected of being inside the shadowy circle of steroid sale or usage. There were certainly enough people arguing that.

My position was somewhat justified a few days later. A brief email from the *New York Times*, coming to me just before I left for baseball's winter meetings, asked me to write an op-ed piece on the same subject. I'd have only seven hundred words—still, it's the *New York Times*. The outcry was the same from the masses who read that paper as it had been from my sabermetrically oriented home at Baseball Prospectus—the issue was never about science, it was about emotion.

Baseball is a game that sparks passion, and any attempt to change the game, for almost any reason, meets a nearly universal blockade. The specter that has been presented to fans—that steroids have somehow changed the game—has never been scientifically tested. For me, that's the necessary gold standard of proof, and it should be used with a healthy skepticism for conventional wisdom.

The lesson of the best-selling *Moneyball* was that too many times in baseball we're all fooled by "our lyin' eyes," as the author Michael Lewis argued. In the case of performance-enhancing drugs, it's not just our eyes, it's also our hearts and minds. Assumption is the marshal of this parade. Fact is stuck somewhere in the back of the ranks. The process I went through in writing this book was one of discovery. I came to the subject with an open mind and a notebook full of questions.

The issue of steroids—which has become shorthand for performance-enhancing drugs, or PEDs—is one filled with complications. Nothing is simple. While some observers attempt to make it so, there is no black or white. The issue is Technicolor, as vivid as life itself. The characters are deep and interesting and flawed, even the good guys. There are as many true believers as you'll find in any war, unwilling to flinch or shift from their entrenched positions.

There is only grey, it seems, when discussing performance-enhancing drugs. Reducing them to simplistic arguments is all too easy, evidenced by the lack of rational, reasoned, and informed discussion in the media. It's much easier for the well-coiffed man in the thousand-dollar suit to scream "Players are on steroids!" than it is to do the research and explain the nuances of prohormone supplementation, controlled-substances legislation, and the base of scientific research for anabolic and androgenic agents.

I've often considered trying one of those thousand-dollar suits. It seems so much easier than this.

I brought in the best people I knew to help in the areas that were beyond my expertise. Getting people like Dr. Kyle Serikawa, a geneticist from the University of Washington, to talk about genetics; or Keith Scherer, a recognized defense attorney, to talk about federal law, made it easier on me. Rather than learning about new subjects, I could concentrate on getting a holistic look at the issue.

The process has taught me more than I expected and taken my thinking in directions I never considered initially. It's a journey that I believe you should now take, hopefully learning more about the facts that will allow for a reasoned discussion of the issue. It's difficult to remove emotion entirely from the discussion when you talk with sixteen-year-olds who are injecting themselves with growth hormone, or when you sit down with men who are brewing up drugs in their basement. Still, they have things to teach us.

I hope you'll open your mind as you read with me. My only hope is to make the game I love and the world I live in a better place.

Note: Throughout the book I have attempted to protect those who requested anonymity by changing their names or making other nonmaterial changes. In order to get to the facts, sometimes it requires a compromise.

WILL CARROLL

A NOTE FROM WILLIAM L. CARROLL, ED.D.

I *did* want to write this book. As a professor and director of the Athletic Training Education Program at the University of Mobile, I deal every day with the types of problems described in these pages. Worse, I know that I'm sending my students into a world where they will have to deal with the problems that performance-enhancing drugs cause for medical professionals.

While I've contributed to many textbooks dealing with both performance-enhancing drugs and illegal drugs and their impact on sports, that isn't enough. The information is not making it through the system. In fact, the system is broken. It is concerned more with catching the few, spending no time and less money on an education program that could actually help.

There's an endless cat-and-mouse game that goes on between drug users and drug testers. What we've failed to do is use the mousetraps available to us. The best mousetrap is simple fact, beautiful knowledge. Few or no facts are being applied now. The media would rather wave their hands in mock horror or indignation than try to solve a problem. Solutions don't make the front pages.

What you read in this book won't solve the problem. Think of it as turning on the faucet. There's a flood of knowledge just waiting to burst forth. There's an army of people that want to see this problem handled, brought under control, and dealt with intelligently. Good men and women are trying to prevent the next Ken Caminiti or the next Steve Bechler.

If you think those tragedies aren't in the works, it is in fact worse. We know those names only because they are professional athletes. The names Sean Riggins, Mike Hegstrand, and Taylor Hooton aren't familiar, but their deaths—blamed on performance-enhancing drugs—are every bit as important as any other. Their deaths count too.

I can remember standing ringside at an event in 1995 where Mike Hegstrand—you might remember him as "Road Warrior Hawk," a professional wrestler—fought in front of a hundred people in rural Missouri. He wore the same makeup and modified shoulder pads that he'd worn years before in front of a full Pontiac Silverdome. His biceps were just as large, bigger than a normal man's thigh. During the match I could almost see his heart pumping in his chest. His heavy breathing and hard sweat, if not the massive muscles and veins, gave him away. I wondered, if I looked closer, in places I didn't want to look, would I see the track marks?

I didn't say anything to Hegstrand that night. He was a grown man, a professional athlete in his own way, and he made his own choices. I tried to ignore the kids in the stands who cheered when he hit his opponents. I tried to ignore the way his veins throbbed in his neck. I wish I hadn't.

When I heard that Hegstrand had died at age forty-six of cardiac problems, I didn't need to know much more. Consider this book an expression of what I meant to say a decade ago.

WILLIAM L. CARROLL, ED.D.

1

Defining the Issue

LET'S START WITH a simple statement that will clarify anything you might be confused about later in this book: I believe that any substance that gives any player an unfair advantage should be banned from use in baseball.

That's the last time we'll be able to say something so simple on this issue. Still, it's important to keep in mind. I believe that most people would agree with the position. It gives us a base for talking about the drug issue intelligently. Try, for a moment, to forget that we're talking about baseball at all. This discussion is equally relevant to any sport, from football to curling.

The issue has been trending down in our society, moving from athletes at the elite level to athletes at the high school level. The problems of Olympic-level competitors are high profile, but farther down the chain there is less knowledge and oversight all around. In other words, I wouldn't want an Olympic sprinter using steroids, but I sure wouldn't want Johnny Quarterback who lives down the street to have steroids that he bought off some guy at the gym.

We'll discuss the scientific definition of steroids in a later chapter, but for now let's look at how the term is used in the ongoing public discussion. The term "steroids" has become the generic. In discussing any drug use in baseball, the media and the general public most often use the simple "steroids" instead of the more accurate term, performance-enhancing drugs. But PEDs encompass far more than just steroids.

Performance-enhancing drugs include, but are not limited to, anabolic and androgenic agents. "Anabolic" refers to a process by which living cells convert simple substances into more complex compounds, especially into living matter. "Androgenic" means that the substance produces masculine characteristics. These agents include steroids, amphetamines, and other substances that create an artificial "up" effect, and drugs that change body processes in such a way as to alter performance positively. It's not just a stronger, faster, or higher response that defines a PED. It can also be enhanced recovery, reduced pain, or increased sensation. The term "ergogenic" is synonymous with PED.

PEDs, however, are not always what you may think. Take, for instance, a drug that for the past five years or so has become one of the most abused drugs in sports. Doctors, both of the medical and witch varieties, purport that it has miracle-healing abilities when injected into aching joints. They also use it to stimulate muscle growth. While you can't get this drug without a prescription, it's easy to come by it at "reasonable" street prices. Taken improperly, a person using this drug could be sent into shock, and deaths have been recorded due to misuse.

The simple solution would be to ban this drug: keep it out of circulation and away from athletes and anyone else who might use it. What is the drug? Insulin. Millions of diabetics lead a normal life because of its easy availability. It is also misused as an ergogenic aid or in a new, controversial healing technique called prolotherapy.

When does a lifesaving drug become an illegal performance-enhancing drug? That's a question for the ethicists, but I'll go as far as saying that the difference lies in intent. Many athletes are also diabetics, and barring them the use of insulin would severely damage their quality of life. Given a choice—their insulin or their sport—few if any would choose sport, certainly if they were given that choice early in life.

The term we should use, then, for drugs that have been determined to offer an unfair competitive advantage or have a deleterious effect on health, should be *illegal performance-enhancing drug*, or IPED for short. And a government or sport sanctioning body should confirm this illegal status.

Let's look at a couple of examples of IPEDs—androstendione and THG, two substances well known to baseball fans. Androstendione was the substance used by Mark McGwire during his 1998 season. Many believe that "andro," because it is something from which testosterone is formed, has anabolic properties—in other words, it helps grow muscle. While current scientific investigation is unclear, and its performance-enhancing properties are in question, there is no question that in 1998, at the time McGwire was using the substance, it was legal under the standards enforced by Major League Baseball. Andro was illegal in many other sports and in the Olympics, but for McGwire it was legal to use. (The recent change in baseball's drug policy now meshes more closely with the federal Anabolic Steroid Control Act, which makes any substance illegal that is "closely related to or with substantially similar effects to a known anabolic steroid.")

THG, on the other hand, was "legal" for a different reason. Because it was an unknown substance, it could not be placed on a list of banned substances. Perhaps a drug called ZZZ will be created and distributed in 2010. Until that drug exists, it cannot be banned.

While technically "legal," then, users of THG, known or unknown, were skirting the rules of the sport. The recent changes by sanctioning bodies and by governments have closed the loophole slightly, tightening the guidelines. Nonetheless this issue again falls to ethics rather than science. Cheaters will cheat; that's what distinguishes them.

By defining these drug terms, we risk painting ourselves into a corner. Just as insulin can be both lifesaving and performance enhancing, many can find grey areas in the use of almost any drug, forcing us back to the intent of the abuser rather than the potential of the drug itself. Insulin, to Jason Johnson, a diabetic pitcher for the Detroit Tigers, is performance enhancing only in that it allows him to be healthy enough to compete athletically. I have seen no one complain that he or any of the other diabetic athletes have a competitive advantage.

Another drug that lives in this PED grey area is Strattera. Manufactured by Eli Lilly and Company in Indianapolis, Strattera is used for attention deficit / hyperactivity disorders (ADHD). It is one of the first nonstimulant drugs used for this condition. Yes, that means that other ADHD drugs, such as Ritalin, have an amphetamine-like effect on abusers. While Strattera is reported to have no "upper" effect, many players feel it gives them better concentration. "They feel 'locked in' and ready to go," said one major league team physician.

While the actual effects of Strattera for non-ADHD sufferers are debatable, its use by athletes points up the fact that they will take almost anything if they think it can give them an advantage. Most will attempt to stay within the rules. Those who feel aided by such drugs will often try to obtain a legitimate prescription from an enabling physician. Major League Baseball has instituted procedures to reduce this practice, forcing players who use such drugs under a new, nonstanding prescription to get a second opinion from an ADHD specialist.

This oversight does not come cheap. Teams are forced to expend both monetary and personnel resources to combat the use of both PEDs and IPEDs. Some teams have gone as far as to bring in psychologists and employee assistance (EAP) counselors. One team actually issued a uniform to its EAP counselor, allowing him to walk on the field and talk with players without drawing attention to that conversation.

The misuse of the term "steroid" extends even to the now-famous BALCO case. Two substances in that case have become all too commonly referred to by the media as the "cream" and the "clear." Yet few if any reporters have described these substances. According to most press reports, BALCO distributed these two substances to athletes, and some also received modanifil, a prescription drug more commonly known as Provigil. Modanifil is a powerful drug that allows some people to stay awake for thirty hours or more without the side effects of amphetamines.

BALCO's "cream" is in fact not a steroid. It is a concentrated version of a prescription testosterone gel. Marketed as Androgel, this cream in its normal version is intended for people with low testosterone counts. Since testosterone is the "gold standard" for steroids, this gel, especially the altered version used by BALCO, can be very effective. It soaks into the skin in the same way nicotine does from a patch. Reports that some users were rubbing it on joints rather than muscles indicate that they may not have fully understood what they were taking or how to use it.

The "clear" is THG, the designer steroid that has caused so much consternation across the sports world. Again, we'll get into the chemistry and politics of THG later, but there is little doubt that it was in fact a steroid. What's more, it was specifically designed to be undetectable by modern testing techniques. For those who wanted to use a steroid but were concerned about drug tests, the "clear" was the ultimate. Oddly, the "clear" isn't clear; it's a medium-brown liquid that looks more like watered-down maple syrup. It also surprised many people that it is not injected. THG is taken orally. BALCO was noted to use flaxseed oil as a delivery agent.

Why flaxseed oil? According to several studies, and as widely reported in the steroid underground, flaxseed oil can counteract some of the estrogenic effects of steroid use, such as the growth of breasts in men. A suspension of THG in flaxseed oil would not only not raise any suspicions (it's sold in health-food stores as a cure-all), it would actually have a purpose. The one concern is that, according to many researchers, the dosing would be problematic since THG is difficult to distribute in the flaxseed oil. This means that even "shaken well," the THG could come in "clumps" or not at all in any given swig.

Advocates of steroid use—yes, there are some—prefer the term AAS (anabolic-androgenic steroid) to PED. It differentiates drugs such as Winstrol, Dianabol, and others that do meet the strict definition of drugs with chemical similarities to testosterone (AAS drugs) from those without such similarities. In the case of supplements, prohormones (substances from which hormones are formed), and so-called designer drugs, this is an important distinction.

Having defined PEDs and IPEDs, we must now consider two other categories: prescription drugs and supplements. Both are legal and controlled under various rules and regulations. Prescription drugs are, obviously, limited by their accessibility, prescribed by physicians and a few other affiliated health professionals for certain approved conditions. Supplements also fall under the FDA but tend to be less regulated, being sold over the counter in health-food and even grocery stores.

Both prescription drugs and supplements have legitimate purposes. Many prescription drugs save lives or raise the quality of life for millions. This $235 billion industry does research and marketing of basic and advanced medical compounds for thousands of conditions. But precription drugs can be as easily abused as any others. It's not always as simple as, say, a radio host getting multiple doctors to write prescriptions for hundreds of opiate pills. In

2003, for instance, Oakland A's pitcher Mark Mulder suffered a hip fracture. In efforts to get him back on the mound in time for the playoffs, the A's are reported to have used the drug Forteo to speed his healing. Forteo is approved for the treatment of osteoporosis in older women. Mulder meets none of these criteria, yet he was reported to have taken the drug with good results. Recently Forteo was also reportedly used with excellent results by the football player Terrell Owens, who was able to play in the Super Bowl only weeks after fracturing his ankle.

Other prescription drugs include growth hormones (used for helping underheight adolescents), insulin (for diabetics), steroids (for cancer patients and AIDS sufferers, among many other uses), and erythropoietin (for anemic chemotherapy patients). All have legitimate medical uses, and all are easily abused when taken for nonmedical, performance-enhancing purposes.

This so-called debate over performance-enhancing drugs has not been much of a debate at all. Most times it has been an emotional plea or political grandstanding. What has been missing is the real information, the facts, that will allow us to have a substantive debate.

I don't start out to belittle anyone's views. I often have to make my position on performance enhancers very clear, as I did at the beginning of this chapter, because I'm willing to listen to all sides and present their ideas, even as something of a devil's advocate.

Framing a debate is often a matter of language. Entire books have been written about choosing words carefully, and most of the terms in this particular debate are loaded (no pun intended). "Drugs" alone carries a massive negative connotation in our society, despite the widespread use of prescription drugs. "Steroids" are bad (and often misused as a word) in sports, yet hormone replacement and anti-aging therapies are a growth field in medicine.

Now that we have common language and an open mind, it's time to dig into the issues.

2

Profile: The Player

"I JUST WANTED to make it."

It was that simple for John Albertson (not his real name). From the time he was six years old, John wanted nothing more than to be a ballplayer. In fact, there was nothing else he could do well. He'd never planned for any life outside of baseball. That confidence, bordering on delusion, gave him the courage to stand in against ninety-mile-an-hour fastballs.

"I have a hit off Roger Clemens."

He'd dreamed of this as a boy, finally fulfilling it in late 2002. He didn't sleep the night after that hit. Instead of going out and partying as many might expect, he spent most of the night talking to his wife halfway across the country. The rest of the night he spent talking to his dad. His dad had been with him at his first game and kicked himself for not going to that night's game. It was just another game, but if he'd known that his Johnny might face Roger Clemens, everything would have been worth it. He'd have taken a vacation day and spent some of the Christmas money he'd been saving for John's son.

"I started taking steroids after the 2001 season."

That was just as simple, just as clear as anything else in John's life. He didn't think about right or wrong. He didn't think about consequences. He didn't think about risks. He thought a lot about that hit off Roger Clemens. In fact, when we spoke over a big stack of pancakes at one of his favorite restaurants, the conversation would circle back from the oddest directions to that one hit. The first words of his son, just three years old and his eyes as big as baseballs, were probably "Roger Clemens."

John had fought like hell to hold on to his dream, well beyond the point where many give up and take workaday jobs and wonder what might have been. He got his first real attention after raising his batting average in Single-A by fifty points. He was older than most of the kids he played against, the ones he saw *Baseball America* writing about. "I could hit 'em," he said. John had a near delusional confidence when he talked about his hitting—a confidence that is both admirable and a little unreal.

The cracks in his confidence came from inside baseball. As he played better, as he got more hits—doing the job he was asked to do—he was also told that he was getting the wrong kinds of hits. "It's an empty .300," a scout told him. The hits were singles, and on a stat sheet, singles without doubles and homers look to a scouting director like flares, squibs, and, worse, flukes. John could get hits all day, but to do more than play in the minors he needed power.

There may be no scientific evidence that physical strength and power hitting have any correlation, but John didn't check the scientific journals in his search for power. "I tried uppercutting more, trying just to get the ball up in the air. All that did was get me more flyouts. They still stayed in the park," he told me. "Then I got serious with the weights. I'd never been much of a lifter to that point because I'd never needed it. I probably wasn't in that gym two weeks before someone approached me."

It wasn't another player who came to John about steroids; it was a muscle-head. "I don't even know if he knew I was a ballplayer.

He probably did. I always wore [team] gear when I was in there." It started casually. Two guys lifting weights and talking about goals. "He just asked if I was trying to bulk up, and I said sure. Maybe he could tell I was frustrated or desperate." More likely, he just saw someone who might be buying what he was selling.

"The guy had what I wanted. Big biceps, barrel chest. Man, that's what looks strong." When the stranger—John doesn't even remember his name—offered him some supplements, John jumped. He knew about things like creatine and andro, but some of the more technical concoctions were a bit more off the mainstream path. John bought DHEA and a couple of other supplements, but another few weeks passed without significant gains before steroids entered the conversation.

"He just mentioned one day that it was something I should think about. It'd get me through a plateau, he said. I didn't need to use much to see the gains." I asked John if he thought much about the minor league drug testing policy, which at that time was much stronger than the major league rules. "No, I didn't even think about it. Not once. I knew it, I guess, but it didn't slow me down."

"I handed him the cash and he stuck me," John told me. He didn't remember how much he paid—maybe fifty bucks—but he did remember making sure he got a clean needle. "It was more important to me that he was using one right out of the packet than what was in the needle. I never once asked what it was. I knew it was steroids, or at least I thought it was."

Talks with gym patrons and law-enforcement officials in the gym area reveal that "Deca" is the leading suspect in John's first injection. Despite the crudeness of Deca compared with other anabolics, it's still the most easily accessible. When I explained to John what I thought he'd taken, he didn't care. "Look, if you told me shooting bull piss was going to get me ten more home runs, fine."

John saw the gains in the gym. "My biceps were bigger, and I just felt . . . not better, that's not the right word. I guess it was confident, but that's not it either." I wasn't going to try to explain the placebo effect or teach John about psychosomatic reactions. The look on his face told me all I needed to know.

"I got to spring training and started off slow. I'd been lifting, not swinging. Forget power, I wasn't hitting period." But the slump didn't stop John from finding more steroids. "I had to find an edge now, and it wasn't hard to find." Another player, a level above him, was able to get him a new vial and some needles. "I hid it from my wife at first. That was probably the worst of it. It didn't feel right not telling her. We'd gone through everything else together."

John's new steroid was Dianabol, sold over the counter in Mexico. "A lot of the guys live in Arizona or southern California in the off-season, and they'll just run down to TJ [Tijuana] for their shit." The needles were easy to find. "Just tell the pharmacist your wife is diabetic. They never check."

The Dianabol wasn't widely used. The one or two guys in the organization who used it weren't as "helpful" as John's original supplier. But "I didn't really have a problem with the injections. I knew more or less how much to take, and that was pretty much it." He never connected his use to a subsequent hamstring injury. "That killed spring for me," he said. "I'd hoped to make an impression, show them the power they kept telling me they wanted to see. . . ." Who was they? I asked. "Scouts and coaches. They never made any secret about the fact that I needed to poke it harder. I can remember [a major league coach] telling me that I hit like a leadoff guy but didn't have the speed. That stung."

John was always negatively motivated. He saw an opposing scouting report that his defense was poor, so he'd spend hours taking pop-ups and grounders at both corners of the infield. The comparison to a weak-hitting speedster was more than enough to blow through any hesitancy he might have had about steroids. Of course, he didn't have much of that to begin with.

"I'd take a bit more every day when I was on my cycles. I read about stacking [the use of two or more steroids to enhance their effect], but I couldn't figure out how to spend more without [my wife] asking questions. On a minor league salary and the little we'd saved in the off-season, a hundred bucks or so a week showed up." How did he save money? "I ate at the ballpark more. Lots of sandwiches from the spread and the snacks they always have. I was leaning up anyway," he said, referring to the fat loss that often accompanies early steroid usage, "so I didn't notice."

On top of the steroids, John was neglecting his nutrition and doing what "all the other players" did. "Popping beans [amphetamines or similar pills]? Well, yeah," he said, looking at me with the same face he might have made had I asked if he was breathing. "You show up at the park and drink your coffee. It's free. Then one of the guys will have some beans before you head out and stretch." Add in some painkillers he was taking to get over lingering soreness in his hamstring and John was a toxic mess.

"I ended up jumping a level from where I thought I would be, because some vet got hurt. By June it got to the point where I thought I might get a shot at The Show." Looking at his stats, not much had changed in John's game. He was still hitting for a high average, but those same scouts would mutter about "empty hits." Whatever power the juice had given him wasn't translating into more extra-base hits.

"I'd get a double and think, 'This is what I worked this off-season for,' but when I got a single, I wouldn't say that I should stop, just that I had to do more." It was a circular descent typical of players I spoke with, a cognitive dissonance that kept their failings their own. Considering his change in minor league level, there was little difference in his stats between 2002 and 2003. The power that steroids promised never showed.

What did change was the way John's muscles worked. He spent the entire season sore and dehydrated. "I couldn't drink enough, it seemed like. It only got worse if I'd go out with the guys and drink a couple. I'd spend the whole next morning pissing and trying to drink water." That dehydration was likely the result of creatine powder that John mixed into his protein shakes. "Without the needle to keep me feeling locked in, the mix was keeping me going. I'd be in after games working out to keep what I'd put on, and there's no doubt that you can recover faster when you're on the mix."

Having already strained his hamstring in spring training, John dealt with an oblique strain throughout much of the season. "It sapped some power, I'm sure," he said, perhaps thinking of it as another explanation for the power that never quite came. At the end of the minor league season, he strained his groin too. "That one almost cost me my shot. I told the trainer, and he told someone at the big club. My agent had to get involved to make sure I got my September call-up."

John did get his call-up and made his debut in his hometown. "That was perfect. A bunch of family and friends got to come see it." He didn't have a hit his first game, but he did get on base by way of a walk. An intentional walk. It was a week later, in mid-September, when he was put into a game late and faced Clemens, getting the hit that so neatly defines him in his own mind. It wasn't a double, only a broken-bat single that lofted just over the third baseman's head.

"I just got the bat on it. I think it was a splitter, and it kind of rode in on me. I was strong enough to kind of carry it out even though the stick split on me. If I could have got better wood on that, it would have been gone." The smile he gets telling this story—and I've heard it ten times if I've heard it once—is infectious. Much like the rash he got the next off-season.

"Of course I got back on it," John said. "I got cut because—guess what—they told me I didn't hit enough to play a corner. I knew that going into spring training I'd need to be stronger. I'd have a new team, a whole new organization to prove something to. I was going to be older than everyone, and no one called me a prospect. No one cared that I'd played in The Show, and no one cared that I hit .300 in Triple-A. They were looking for a fourth outfielder with some pop."

The rash was mild at first, near where he injected himself. "It was the first time [my wife] really noticed. I got out of the shower and she saw the red spots and she made me go to the doctor." His wife had been doing medical-records clerking during the off-season, and she had learned enough to tell John that he had a staph infection. It was cleared up easily, and the doctor whom John saw at an immediate-care center was overworked enough to ignore obvious needle marks. He wrote the prescription and moved on to the next examining room, to a coughing child or a sick nine-to-fiver. John wasn't a big leaguer to the doctor, but the doctor enabled him just the same.

John learned from his mistake of the previous year, combining hitting drills with his workouts and, once again, cycles of Dianabol. "I went down to TJ myself, more to save money than anything else. I knew if I bought it off someone, they were lining their pockets a little bit. One guy I bought from would draw a couple full syringes off and put it in his own vial before he sold it to you. He didn't jack the price up, he just took some for himself."

John appears normal. He looks like an athlete I guess, but you could pass him on the street and not look twice, as you would at a massive NFL lineman or a towering NBA player. He doesn't have unnatural dimensions or the classic signs of steroid usage. His brow doesn't protrude, his jaw is normal. Even when it comes to side effects, it's not clear that steroids did anything for John.

"I went into that camp with [the new team] strong. I felt really good, but we'd had some problems during the winter." One side effect that John didn't avoid was the moodiness and quick temper that steroid users are known for. His wife had pushed him to take the best offer, coaxing him from his longtime agent to a bigger agency. The new agent brought him to a new hitting coach and adjusted his swing. By the time he made it to camp in February, he was already hurt.

"The new guy had me torquing, and that got my back sore, so I'd just pop some pills to get out there. It ended up working against me." In just the second week of camp, doctors found a herniated disc. One doctor also noticed the scars from the earlier rash. "He pulled me aside and asked if I'd been taking anything. I didn't know this guy, so I said no. He didn't buy it and said I should talk to one of the strength and conditioning guys. I never did."

John had talked through two full seasons of steroid usage with me and I hadn't heard him mention a single drug test. When I asked him about it, he just laughed. "Sure, we had a couple, but we just cheated those. We'd know they were coming, and it wasn't too hard to get things by the tester. Everybody had his tricks. I'd just hand the guy a Bennie [a hundred dollars] and that was that. It was a lot cheaper than taking a suspension."

Back in Triple-A for another season, things went downhill rapidly for John. "It was just the wrong situation there. I could never get comfortable, and my wife and kid weren't there until mid-May. My back kept acting up, and my knee started hurting. I was spending more time in the trainer's room than I ever had. Worse, I didn't really get close to anyone on the team. I ran up one heck of a cellular bill, and if you'd paid me by the hit I couldn't have paid it off."

John had spent the previous three seasons as a hitting machine, consistently cranking out .300 averages at every level. Two months into repeating the same level, something that's supposed to be easier, John found his average hovering around .200. And the power he'd been promised by drugs still had not been delivered.

"I was pressing by this point," he said, going through the box scores he saves from every game. "I couldn't run because of my knee, so I wasn't able to play the outfield. I had to try and play first when I could, but the team wanted to keep their prospect playing, so I'd DH some or just pinch hit. As my average dropped, so did my time. Eventually I couldn't buy a chance to break out of it."

John walked into the manager's office in early June knowing that he was headed out. He'd expected to be sent down to Double-A, but the team elected to release him. It was the first time he'd been cut since junior high. "I had a week before my agent was able to find me another slot, and I really thought about just going home. If I'd had the money to do it, I really think I would have. My wife was pregnant again, so getting back on with a team was more important. Luckily I was able to get back into [his previous] organization. The rest of the season I just did what I did before, and you know what? The scouts said the same things."

Before the 2004 season, John and his wife, now parents of two small children, sat down and talked about his steroid usage. She'd known pretty much all along what he was doing and often debated whether or not to say something. She actually felt guilty talking about it now.

"Should I have said something?" she asked, more to herself than me. "I didn't tell anyone because I didn't know what it really was. I tried to find stuff on the internet, but most of it was either 'get big now' or 'say no to drugs' kind of stuff that I didn't know which end was up. None of the other wives and girlfriends ever mentioned their guys using anything. It's something we just didn't talk about.

"We're a team, and I think I supported him, but I wish I'd done more. He could have been one of those guys you see on the news with a heart attack rather than home playing with his kids. What I couldn't do is tell him what it took to play. I've heard how many players take things."

It's an open question: How many players in the minor leagues are on some substance?

John gets defensive when I ask that question. "If I give you an answer, you have to look at me and say why I'm telling you. If I say everyone's doing it, it's just to make me feel better because *I* did, isn't it? If I say it's low, you'll just think I'm protecting my friends.

"The truth of the matter is, I don't know. Most of the guys take something. We're all on creatine or zinc or some supplement, and drinking EAS [a popular protein drink]. There's always something around to get you up for a game, but a lot depends on the clubhouse. Juice or something illegal? [It was interesting how he separated the two.] I guess it was 'don't ask, don't tell.' If I didn't ask them, they wouldn't ask me. I didn't go around thinking this guy does this or that guy takes that. It's just not how things work.

"At worst, someone might tell me about something. There was one guy who had a bunch of ADD drugs that he'd gotten from one of the batboys. That stuff was just like speed. But it never got to a stage where anyone would push me to try something or where we'd do much to get it. It was more like grabbing the low-hanging fruit, taking what was there."

John spent a third season in Triple-A. In 2005 he was hoping to be back again, if he could make it through spring training. "My knees have gotten progressively worse. Age, man." In fact, it might not be age. John has patellar tendonitis, a condition often considered a side effect of steroid usage. What he never got was the power he wanted so desperately. It was a bloop single he hit off Clemens, not a home run.

While John's story is his own, it's hardly unique. Neither is it rampant. Discussions with players and baseball officials lead me to think that there is a relatively low level of steroid usage in the minor leagues, somewhere below 10 percent. The level of usage for other drugs is significantly higher. Uppers appear to have near universal usage once things like ephedra, caffeine tablets, and prescription ADD drugs are included with amphetamines. Tolerance for cocaine is near zero, though reports of usage still exist.

Two major league players tested positive while part of the U.S. Olympic baseball qualifying team. It's a fact that few baseball followers know. Fewer still can name these two players who tested positive for a banned anabolic steroid. Derrick Turnbow and Terrmel Sledge didn't face much of an outcry when they made the loop through their respective leagues. No one held up signs or discussed their eligibility, mostly because it is not an affront to the "integrity of the game" that two marginal prospects tested positive.

It is important to note that while both players tested positive under the Olympic program, it is also reasonable to assume that neither tested positive as part of the minor league testing program. Neither served a suspension, begging the question of how effective the minor league testing program is at detection. The substance they used, nandrolone, is one of the most available and easily tested anabolic steroids.

In 2003 and 2004 the best available estimate of positive tests in the minor leagues is thirty. The number is likely higher, due to first offenders being placed on an "administrative track" for most substances. Both major league and minor league officials refused to confirm the numbers obtained. If four unknown violators accompany each known violator (a fair rule of thumb in this business), the percentage of minor league violators comes in below but similar to the 5 percent found in the 2003 major league survey testing.

There is also significant abuse of painkillers at all levels of baseball. The story of top prospect Jeff Allison, a first-round pick of the Florida Marlins, and his addiction to the prescription drug OxyContin scared many in baseball that more pressure would come to bear on narcotic use.

"I'm in pain all the time," said a major league player who fought through injury last season while putting up big numbers. "Every son of a bitch in here is on something. Aspirin, Advil, Vioxx, whatever. I have to get spiked [injections of painkillers] just to get on the field."

There was little outcry when Gary Sheffield took several cortisone shots to make it through a shoulder injury. It was certainly nothing compared to the jeers that Jason Giambi, his New York Yankee teammate heard when his health problems, possibly steroid related, kept him off the field for the better part of the 2004 season.

Curt Schilling, the hero of the Boston Red Sox World Series win in 2004, made it through the season on an injured ankle through the use of Marcaine, a local anesthetic that he had injected into his ankle both before and during games. Without the drug, Schilling would likely not have been able to pitch much of the season and certainly would not have been on the mound with blood seeping through his sock. For the few who may not know this late-model myth, Schilling had a surgical procedure to hold his dislocated tendon in place (albeit not the normal anatomic position) twice during the playoffs.

The aches and pains that come with a 162-game schedule create a need for anti-inflammatories, painkillers, and other drugs that aid recovery and healing. The usage is much less than in football, a game that covets the collision. In that sport, painkiller injections are commonplace on the sidelines, being reported vividly in H. G. Bissinger's seminal high school football story, *Friday Night Lights*. As the collisions get more violent and the injuries more severe, the usage ramps up in frequency and dosage.

"Guys get hit so hard, they literally have the feces knocked out of them," one former player, Merrill Hoge, told *ESPN Magazine*. Baseball has no such common collisions, only occasionally, or a fearsome beaning. It's the persistent aches and pains, combined with the common need to raise dosages as the body adjusts to consistent drug use, that worries players. "I've seen what happens to people that are on these for long terms," said one major league player. "Isn't this what they think forced Alonzo Mourning [an NBA player] to need a new kidney?"

While increasing dosages and more severe effects are one problem, it is the shift from nonsteroidal anti-inflammatory drugs (NSAIDs) to narcotics that is more worrisome. "I know guys that are out there goofy," one former major leaguer told me. "They're taking something to take the edge off whatever's aching them, then they're taking something to put the edge back on, and on top of that they're supposed to be sleeping normal hours, so they might as well pop a pill for that too."

Recent research on NSAIDs is interesting. It suggests that much of the effect may be purely mental and the rest may be due to the mild analgesic properties of the drug. In a presentation at the American Sports Medicine Institute's yearly convention, an osteopath presented research showing that the effect of NSAIDs might depend entirely on analgesic effect rather than any real anti-inflammatory properties.

Million-dollar athletes are seldom recipients of any measure of pity. Not once did John Albertson ask me for sympathy or offer an apology. While he put as little thought into steroid use as is humanly possible, he accepts the consequences just as he cherishes that hit against Clemens. In fact, "John" wanted to use his real name in this piece.

"My agent won't let me. I'm having a hard enough time finding a job at my age," he told me. "Looking at the crap that's come down on Giambi, it's just not worth it. I can't lose it this year. We have kids."

It's almost ironic what John hopes to do when he retires. "I'd hoped to save more toward setting myself up. I think owning a GNC [a leading health-food and supplement chain] would be best. I know about all the stuff, and I think people in my hometown would remember me as a professional athlete. That's got to help with sales, I'd think."

He's already got the picture picked out for display behind the counter. You guessed it—it's him at bat against Roger Clemens.

3

A Brief History of
Performance-enhancing Drugs

THE USE OF performance-enhancing drugs in sports is as old as sport itself. Dr. Augustin Mendoza, a sports medicine expert, believes that the use of performance-enhancing substances probably began when some caveman found a mysterious root and, after chewing it, had a very successful day of hunting, was named leader of his clan, and was rewarded with the sleeping area in the cave closest to the fire. Soon other cavemen were searching for similar roots to chew on to make them better hunters.

In order to understand the concept of performance enhancement, one must first have two basic definitions. First, the accepted definition of a "drug" is any chemical substance that affects human physiology or psychology. Second, sport has been defined by Webster as "an active diversion requiring physical exertion and competition." While the definition of a drug is satisfactory and utilitarian, the definition of sport encompasses many areas that do not fit our current conception of sport.

"Festival fighters" in ancient Greece and gladiators in the Roman Empire can be considered among the earliest recorded athletes. As early as 800 B.C., Greece sponsored funeral games that included not only combat-type competitions between gladiators but also poetry readings. The Greeks had incorporated sport into the cultural and spiritual activities of their time. Emphasis was placed on the aesthetic nature of athletics and its preparatory role for warriors. Participants were required to display some form of artistic ability as well as perform athletic feats. Athletic competitions were an important means of establishing the economic and political importance of the various regions of the country. This symbiotic relationship between politics and athletics foreshadowed the substance-enhanced "win-at-all-costs" philosophy espoused by many twentieth-century governments.

The ancient Olympics, which lasted from 776 B.C. until 393 A.D., provided a new vehicle for performance-enhancing drugs. Around 780 B.C., Iphitos, a descendant of Oxylos, king of Elis, began his efforts to forge a truce with the kings of Sparta and Pisa, two other Greek city-states, in order to hold a Panhellenic competition at Olympia. The truce not only proclaimed Olympia to be a sanctuary of Zeus but also declared that during the time of the competition, all adverse issues among the parties would be set aside. Athletes would be able to safely travel to and from Olympia in order to compete. In preparation for these Olympics, the participants would arrive a month before the competition. During this time they were to train and eat nothing but cheese and water. But it became widely known that the Spartan "coaches" were supplementing their athletes with various herbs and mushroom concoctions in an effort to give them a competitive edge. These substances mitigated the athletes' pain and essentially made them psychotic. Around 700 B.C. new events were added to the games, making more athletes necessary: a mile and three-mile run, wrestling, and the pentathlon.

The Roman era of sport lacked the gentility of the Greeks. The first recorded Roman gladiatorial games were held in 46 B.C. by Marcus Brutus (who later would fatally stab Julius Caesar) in honor of his father. Not sanctioned by the Republic, the games were quite small.

Most Roman nobles preferred to watch the gladiators perform at the Coliseum, the largest structure of its kind in the ancient world. Roman gladiators were trained at special schools originally owned by private citizens but later taken over by the imperial state to prevent the buildup of a private army. Gladiators trained like true athletes, much as professional athletes do today. They received medical attention and three meals a day.

The day-to-day care of these athletes fell to physicians, most of them neophytes. If a young man wished to become a physician, he would essentially apprentice himself to a physician for up to six months, then hang out his own shingle and begin further on-the-job training. Rufus, who has been credited with naming many parts of the body, and Soranus and Galen, both of whom wrote some of the first books on anatomy, began their medical practices working on gladiators. Crude surgery (without anesthesia) was performed, and often the bodies of fallen gladiators were skinned or boiled so that physicians might study anatomical structures.

Perhaps the most infamous of the Roman physicians was Flanius, a child of the noble class who had the finest medical education of his time and moved in Rome's highest social circles. He had access to information and "souvenirs" from the latest Roman conquests, some of which included captured medical practitioners and plants of various kinds. Flanius picked the brains of the captured medical practitioners and experimented with plants for the express purpose of finding a substance that would enhance the performance of the gladiators he cared for. The plants included coca leaves, hemlock, thistle, and lotus. Since the process of injecting medications had not yet been invented, Flanius's preparations were often mixed with wine to be consumed by the gladiators.

While there is no way today to measure the success or failure or Flanius's preparations, it is known that his stable of gladiators was extremely popular with the Roman crowds. Flanius often boasted to his upper-class friends—who were allegedly heavy bettors on the gladiatorial contests and would have welcomed the information—that his medicinal preparations could turn an average slave into a ferocious and successful Colosseum champion. Sound familiar?

With the fall of the Roman Empire and the dawning of a new era, sporting activities for the entertainment of the masses ended. The only available information about the use of performance-enhancing drugs was limited to their use by soldiers. The "Berserker" Vikings allegedly ingested hallucinogenic mushrooms and potions containing animal blood and alcohol to increase their aggressiveness in battle. These same Vikings, once they had disembarked for battle, would burn their ships so they would have no opportunity for surrender. Stories of the Crusaders who fought for Richard the Lionhearted recount how the knights' servants would spike the mead (a honey wine) with a stimulant-like substance before an anticipated battle.

The first reported death in the world of sport attributed to a performance-enhancing drug occurred in 1896. The Welsh cyclist Andrew Linton died during the Paris-to-Bordeaux cycling race after drinking a substance reported to be trimethyl. Trimethyl is an alcohol-based product allegedly used in long-distance bicycle races to ease pain and add stamina.

Linton's death occurred in France during the same year as the first modern Olympic Games, organized by an aristocratic Frenchman, Baron Pierre de Coubertin. De Coubertin, who wrote the Olympic Oath, was an idealist who foresaw the Olympics as an apolitical gathering of pure athletes where the emphasis would be on competing rather than winning. "The important thing in life is not the triumph, but the struggle" was probably his most famous saying. The Baron died in 1937 before the Olympics became the chemically enhanced, political, and commercial circus it has become today.

The 1904 Olympic marathon proved to be the antithesis of de Coubertin's Olympic ideal. The man who crossed the finish line first, Frederick Lorz of the United States, was later disqualified for riding more than ten miles of the race in his manager's automobile. The eventual declared winner was Thomas Hicks, also of the United States, who had passed out twice during the race, only to be revived with two doses of strychnine-laced brandy.

Other events at about the same time, though apparently overlooked, were to play a role in the future of performance-enhanced sports. In 1889 Charles Édouard Brown-Séquard, a French physiologist, concocted a "rejuvenating therapy for the body and mind." His bizarre elixir was a liquid extract made from the testicles of guinea pigs and dogs. Brown-Séquard claimed that his potion increased physical strength and intellectual prowess.

In 1921, at the University of Chicago, Fred Koch, a chemist, succeeded in isolating the male hormone testosterone. He accomplished this by grinding tons of bulls' testicles and using chemicals to isolate the testosterone. This hormone was then injected into capons (neutered chickens) over a period of six weeks, with the result that the capons began to display definite male characteristics in demeanor, crowing ability, and comb coloration.

In 1931 Adolf F. J. Butenandt isolated testosterone from male urine and thus was able to determine the exact chemical formula of the hormone. In 1935 a Yugoslav chemist working in Zurich, Leopold Rozicka, was able to transform chemical cholesterol into synthetic testosterone using Butenandt's formula. For their accomplishments, Butenandt and Rozika shared the 1939 Nobel Prize for chemistry. Physicians and researchers in Europe immediately began human experiments by injecting synthetic testosterone into males with improperly developed testes—with decided success in most of the reported cases. This synthetic hormone was the grandfather of today's Androgel.

The Berlin Olympics of 1936 were replete with rumors of performance-enhancing drug use by German athletes. There was historical reason for concern. By 1932 sprinters were experimenting with nitroglycerine in an effort to dilate their coronary arteries. Later they began experimenting with Benzedrine, an amphetamine that in those days could be bought over the counter in the form of an inhaler.

But the real modern doping era began with the introduction of injectable testosterone in 1935. Developed by Nazi doctors to promote aggression in their troops, testosterone found its way onto the athletic field with Germany's team for the 1936 Olympics. Olympic winners had allegedly used testosterone preparations before—notably the distance runner Paavo Nurmi with a product called Rejuvin (the same name given to a currently available homeopathic HGH [human growth hormone] spray) in the 1920s. But the German initiative was a quantum leap in the availability of synthetic testosterone. Despite the heroics of the African American Jesse Owens, which greatly embarrassed Adolf Hitler and his "master race" propaganda, the Germans won more Olympic medals than any other country at the Berlin Olympics—eighty-nine compared to the United States' fifty-nine.

In the late 1930s and early 1940s sport took a backseat to World War II. During the war there were reports of rampant use of amphetamines by U.S. soldiers, who took them to stay awake and alert, and the use of testosterone by elite Nazi SS troops. At the end of the war, many German scientists who had been involved in testosterone synthesis escaped to Russia. The work they did in the Soviet Union prepared the way for the proliferation of anabolic steroid use throughout the world of sport for the next sixty-plus years.

In 1942 the team physician of the St. Louis Cardinals directed that regular multi-vitamins (the equivalent of today's Centrum) be given to all the players. The athletic trainer and equipment manager convinced the players that these pills contained "something much more than just vitamins." Whether or not the vitamins were responsible, the Cardinals enjoyed an outstanding year, winning more than one hundred games and capturing the National League pennant. These vitamins may have been one of the best placebo studies in the history of sport.

In the late 1940s the mecca of weight lifting in the United States was the small Pennsylvania town of York, population less than twenty thousand, located about a hundred miles west of Philadelphia. Even though York was once the capital of the United States (for about nine months in 1777–1778, when Philadelphia was under threat of advancing British troops), it was the York Barbell Company, under the direction of Bob Hoffman, that made this town so important in the sport of weight lifting.

Hoffman, a Georgia-born decorated World War I veteran who developed a fanatical interest in barbell weight training in his early thirties, founded his company in 1929. It manufactured barbell and barbell weight plates as well as other weight-lifting accessories, and by 1946 was grossing over a million dollars a year.

Some of Hoffman's employees were elite weight-lifting champions who not only performed services for the company but also comprised the York Barbell Club, the most venerable aggregation of weight-lifting title holders in the history of the United States. Included in this group were world champions Gord Venables, Stan Stanczyk, John Terpark, and Mr. America winners Jules Bacon and John Grimek.

In October 1946 when the York Barbell team defeated the Soviet national team at the World Weight Lifting Championship in Paris, Bob Hoffman's company was a financial success beyond his dreams. Hoffman became one of the most respected men in the world of sports. Among his many friends was Dr. John Ziegler.

Ziegler began his medical practice as a general practitioner in rural Montana. Always an avid sportsman, he eventually became team physician for the United States weight-lifting team. This meteoric rise was in no way hindered by his friendship with Hoffman.

In 1948 the United States had won Olympic gold medals in four of the six weight classifications in weight lifting; in 1952 the U.S. team won gold medals in five of the seven classifications. But the Soviets, returning to the Olympics after a twelve-year absence, won gold in three weight classes (in one class the two countries tied for first place). Ziegler, who was present at Helsinki in 1952, began to see the writing on the wall. It was virtually impossible for a team to post this many Olympic victories after being out of Olympic competition for so long.

Ziegler had heard rumors around the Olympic venues about the Soviet athletes using performance-enhancing drugs, but he had no hard evidence. The trend continued at the 1956 Melbourne Olympics when the United States won gold in four of the seven weight classes while the USSR won the other three gold medals. The gap was narrowing.

The evidence was to hit Ziegler in the face when he served as team physician for the U.S. weight-lifting team at the 1956 world championships in Vienna. There he observed the Soviet team being injected with a substance he believed to be testosterone—perfectly legal at the time. The International Olympic Committee had neither a banned-substances list nor a drug-testing program until 1968.

One of the Soviet coaches (perhaps after one too many vodkas) revealed to Ziegler that the Soviets had been injecting weight lifters and other athletes with testosterone since the mid-1940s. He also told Ziegler that this was possible because of the German scientists who had defected to Russia at the end of World War II and brought their formulas with them. Ziegler now realized that it would be virtually impossible for the U.S. team to compete with the chemically enhanced Russians. He decided it was time to fight fire with fire: the cold war was joined by the chemical warfare of performance-enhancing drugs.

Upon his return to the United States, Ziegler contacted the Ciba Pharmaceutical Company and worked with its scientists to develop an oral anabolic steroid. The work culminated in the development of Dianabol, Ciba's trade name for methandrostenolone, which appeared on the market in 1960. Ciba could produce this product because it had a legitimate use in the treatment of hypogonadism. (Although Ciba ceased production of Dianabol in the 1980s, the product can still be purchased from foreign pharmaceutical companies in Mexico and Belize.)

With access to this new oral anabolic before its official release, Ziegler decided to do some research of his own with members of the York Barbell Club. He dispensed five milligrams per day (the therapeutic dose for individuals with low testosterone production) but soon found that the athletes had found another source and were taking the oral anabolic in much higher dosages. This resulted in the development of some medical pathologies among the athletes, and when Ziegler saw this, he discontinued experimentation with the drug.

It is sadly ironic that Ziegler, who was to become known as the "Father of Anabolic Steroids in the United States," came to regret his role in producing the drug. His dream of leveling the playing field turned into a nightmare. "I wish I'd never heard the word 'steroid,' " he said. "These kids do not realize the price they'll pay."

At the 1960 Olympics in Rome, the first to be widely tele-
vised, athletes became more than names in news reports. They
now had a face. The Soviets launched Sputnik in 1957, and the
"race for space" had become part of the cold war. Even though
U.S. weight lifters now had access to anabolic steroids, the Soviets
took gold in five of the seven weight classes while the United
States won only one. Rome also marked the unveiling of two high-
profile female Soviet athletes who had allegedly added testosterone
to their training regimens. It seemed to be working as Tamara
Press won gold in the shot put and silver in the discus while her
sister Irina was a runaway gold medalist in the eighty-meter hur-
dles. The games were shocked by the death of Knut Enemark
Jensen, a Danish cyclist, who collapsed on opening day while
competing in the hundred-kilometer trial race. The official cause
of death was "sunstroke." But an autopsy revealed that Jensen had
been given a mixture of amphetamines and nicotinyl tartrade.
Amphetamines had been widely used by cyclists, but Jensen's un-
timely death brought the issue to the front pages and marked one
of the early events that prompted the International Olympic
Committee (IOC) to consider drug testing to preserve an image of
integrity in the Olympics.

Another world-class cyclist, Tommy Simpson, died in the
course of the Tour de France in 1967. Tour officials announced
that Simpson's death resulted from a combination of heat and exhaustion, but an autopsy showed that Simpson had traces of amphetamines in his blood. Investigators also discovered more of the
drugs in his hotel room and the pockets of his jersey.

The 1964 Olympics in Tokyo came to be known as the
"Steroid Olympics." Rumors were in the air that the IOC was developing a banned-substances list and a program for drug testing.
In the Olympic village, athletes talked more about drugs than any
other subject. Soviet bloc countries won gold in six of the seven
weight divisions in weight lifting. The United States captured gold

in the shot put while the Soviets took the gold in the hammer throw. Tamara Press won gold in the shot put and discus while Irina won the pentathlon.

The promised drug testing at the 1968 Olympics did occur, but it did little to slow the use of performance-enhancing drugs. Since substances such as anabolic steroids are testosterone based, no test had yet been developed that could differentiate between ingested or injected testosterone and the testosterone that occurs naturally in the human body. The Soviet weight-lifting team took only three gold medals while the U.S. team's only medal was a bronze in the heavyweight division. The Press sisters did not make the trip to Mexico City with the Soviet team even though they had the best performances in the world that year in their events. After 1968 they were never heard from in the world of track and field.

The only violation of the IOC's banned-substance list to be revealed in Mexico City was a Swedish pentathlete, Hans-Gunnar Liljenwall. Liljenwall tested positive for excessive alcohol, and his team (the modern pentathlon is a team event) was disqualified and had to return the medal they had won. In a later explanation to the press, Liljenwall claimed, "I only had two beers to give me a little buzz to relax during the shooting aspect of the pentathlon." IOC drug testing was off to an inauspicious start.

Meanwhile, in the United States, anabolic steroids had found their way to the National Football League. Dazzled by stories about the strength that athletes around the world had accomplished, NFL teams hired strength coaches to develop bigger, stronger athletes, primarily for their offensive and defensive lines. One strength coach was later to say, "When he hired me, the coach told me to make them bigger and stronger and that he didn't care how I did it as long as I got results." American sport could now mark its entry into the steroid age: it was 1968.

What became accepted in the NFL soon became an object of desire at the collegiate and high school levels. This is the "filter down" effect. If bigger and stronger was what it took to win, everyone wanted to take that step. Neither the NCAA nor any state high school governing body had a drug-testing policy at the time, and even if they did, there remained no accurate test for testosterone-based anabolic steroids. The National Basketball Association initiated its drug-testing procedures in 1983. The NCAA did not begin drug testing (and then only for certain sports) until 1986. The NFL began drug testing in 1987. Baseball, of course, has only recently developed a drug-testing program.

The 1972 Olympics at Munich will always be remembered as the Olympics of tragedy, when Arab terrorists stormed the Olympic village and ultimately claimed the lives of eleven Israeli athletes. With the Olympic flag and those of all nations represented flying at half-mast, the Soviets won four of the eight gold medals in weight lifting. The super heavyweight division was won by Vasiliy Alekseyev, a giant of a man who was to break eighty world weight-lifting records in six years. It is alleged that Alekseyev was stacking more than 350 milligrams of anabolic steroids per day at his peak—seventy times the therapeutic dosage.

The highlight of the Olympic drug-testing program in 1972 was the disqualification of the U.S. runner Rick Demont. Demont paid the price for official bungling. He filed the appropriate forms and made officials aware of the asthma medication he was using, and that it contained ephedrine. But the failure of a USOC official to follow through on required procedures caused him to test positive. He was banned from competition and forced to return the gold medal he won in the four hundred meters.

The 1976 Olympics in Montreal showcased the East German women's swim team. After winning five medals at the 1972 Munich games, these large, muscular women with deep voices walked away from Montreal with eleven gold medals of a possible thirteen and put the swimming world on notice that they were unbeatable. None of the winners failed a drug test, but that was because the sport scientists back home had already taken steps to make sure they would pass. At Montreal, too, the Soviets collected seven of nine possible gold medals in weight lifting.

In East Germany there were celebrations by political officials and fans—but not by the swimmers, who were beginning to understand what was being done to them. Forced by physicians, coaches, and other handlers charged with their care to take massive doses of anabolic steroids, the female swimmers were getting bigger and stronger, and posting fabulous times in the pool. They were also developing deep voices, body hair on their torso, severe acne, and other adverse effects of anabolic steroid use. Anabolic steroids have more pronounced androgenous (masculinizing) and androgenic (performance-enhancing) effects on females because their bodies would ordinarily produce only a small amount of testosterone.

To fully appreciate the heinousness of the crimes against these young athletes, one must understand that they were politically motivated. After the division of Germany following World War II, the Communist East Germans had wanted to make a political statement. Like their Soviet counterparts, East Germany chose sport in general and women's swimming in particular as their vehicle to make that statement. Their goals required the complicity of high state officials (including the Ministry of State Security that oversaw the East German Sport Science Bureau), coaches, and even the parents of the young athletes.

The system started with recruiting. State coaches would attend youth sports activities and identify girls who demonstrated athletic potential. They then made the parents of these children an offer they couldn't refuse. If they allowed their daughters to enter the program, take up residence at the Dynamo Swim Club, and train with the team, the children would be well cared for and the parents would be allowed to keep their jobs and not be sent to prison as an enemy of the state. Since there were few prospects for getting ahead in East Germany, many parents thought this program might be a good thing for their children, but they didn't understand why they would not be allowed to visit them regularly once they entered the program. Parents would eventually discover that officials did not want them to see the physical changes that were about to occur in their children.

The primary weapon in the crime was an anabolic steroid known as Oral Turinabol, in blue pills given to the young women as "vitamins." Oral Turinabol was manufactured by VEB Jenapharm, an East German pharmaceutical company that had found an excellent customer willing to purchase all the substance the company could produce. That customer was the East German Sport Science Bureau.

When the East Germans were "tipped off" by a high-ranking IOC authority that a drug test had been developed to reveal anabolic steroid use by determining the ratio of testosterone (injected or ingested) to epitestosterone (naturally occurring in the body), physicians and scientists in the Sports Science Bureau immediately went to work to find a way to beat the test. By giving their athletes both testosterone and epitestosterone, the necessary 6 to 1 ratio could be maintained in order to pass the new test. The East Germans also switched to injectable Testosterone-Depot because it had a shorter half-life (the amount of time it takes the body to get rid of a substance) and thus could be used almost up to the day of competition. This type of subterfuge is still commonly used as a means of beating drug tests in modern sports, especially American professional sports.

The chief physician of the East German doping program, referred to by the athletes as "Dr. Frankenstein," was Manfred Hoppner. After Communist rule ended and records became public, Hoppner was charged with massive illegalities. At his trial, he claimed he was just following the orders of Manfred Ewald, chairman of the East German Sports Commission. This was an interesting revelation since Ewald was president of the East German Olympic Committee that had been awarded a gold medal for its contribution to sport by Juan Antonio Samaranch, then president of the International Olympic Committee.

The East German Sports Bureau went to major lengths to avoid having its athletes disqualified from world and Olympic competitions. It installed its own drug-testing equipment, including a state-of-the-art mass spectrometer and gas chromatograph. Athletes were tested weekly to determine their testosterone/epitestosterone ratio, and tested again immediately before athletes were scheduled to leave the country to compete.

Justice was never done in this case. Ewald and Hoppner, along with seven other doctors, coaches, and trainers (a nebulous term in Europe) were found guilty of the infliction of willful bodily harm on children and fined. There were no jail sentences.

The young German swimmers, now grown, are the ones who are still serving time in a living hell for the crimes against them by the state. Uta Krause testified that she had attempted suicide because of the effects of the drugs on her body and her mind. Rica Reinisch testified of having suffered numerous stomach, gynecological, and psychological problems and severe cardiac damage as a direct result of the doping. Karen Konig testified to severe depression. Martina Gottschalt gave birth to a child with birth defects. The list goes on.

Hopefully there will never be another scandal like the drama of East Germany or even one at the level of the Soviets in the 1950s and 1960s. But as long as there are people greedy for power or money, the potential for abuse exists.

Probably the highest-profile case of doping at the Olympics occurred in 1988 at Seoul, when the Canadian sprinter Ben Johnson was stripped of his gold medal and world record in the hundred-meter dash after testing positive for the anabolic steroid stanozolol. Nearly fifteen years later it was discovered that several

American track athletes had tested positive for drugs before those Seoul games. Allegedly among them was Carl Lewis, who was awarded the gold medal after Johnson's disqualification.

Another unfortunate story is that of Barret Robbins who, as I write this in 2005, lies in a Miami hospital with gunshot wounds from policemen he allegedly tried to attack. The six-foot-three-inch, 360-pound Robbins will always be remembered as the Oakland Raider who went AWOL from the Super Bowl in 2003 and was later located on a drinking and drug binge in Tijuana. Robbins, who has been treated for bipolar personality disorder, also turned up on a customer list belonging to BALCO. If there was ever a person who should not risk the adverse psychological side effects of performance-enhancing drugs, Robbins should be the poster boy.

In 1996 Ken Caminiti of the San Diego Padres was the unanimous choice for National League MVP. Today he is dead, felled by a heart attack at the age of forty-one. The three-time All Star third baseman was often in trouble after his career ended in 2001, and was on probation for a drug offense at the time of his death.

Caminiti later admitted that he had used anabolic steroids during much of his career, including his MVP year. He went on to claim that half the players in the big leagues were using them. Even though steroids had left him with health problems, Caminiti defended his use and said he could not discourage others from using them. "Look at all the money in the game," Caminiti said. "The salaries are through the roof. So I can't say 'don't do it' when the guy sitting next to you is big as a house and he's going to take your job and make the money."

Another former baseball player, Jose Canseco, has estimated that from 80 to 90 percent of major league players use anabolic steroids. Canseco admits that he used them and has named numerous other players who allegedly did too, including Mark McGwire and Rafael Palmeiro. Palmeiro denies using steroids. In his book, Canseco even attempted to implicate President George W. Bush, saying that he must have been aware of his players using steroids when he was boss of the Texas Rangers. Whether or not you choose to believe the percentages stated by Canseco or Caminiti, it is obvious that baseball players have been involved in chemical warfare, seeking the "edge" that will give them an advantage and make them a lot of money.

Recently the BALCO scandal and the "leaks" of grand jury testimony have thrown baseball players into the anabolic limelight. What we can be sure of is that Victor Conte, the founder of BALCO, was a master marketer and networker. He used his friendship with Greg Anderson, Barry Bonds's personal trainer, to hustle clients for both his dietary supplements and designer steroids. He bathed in the limelight and enjoyed his acquaintance with top stars, including Bonds, Jason Giambi, Bill Romanowski of the Oakland Raiders, and track stars Tim Montgomery and Marion Jones.

Conte bragged about being able to develop "chemical cocktails" that would, in conjunction with a heavy resistance weight-training program, not only make an individual bigger and stronger but also fool the drug tests. He was able to deliver on one of two of his promises, but his failure to deliver on the other essentially cost Montgomery the right to compete in the 2004 Olympics, got Kelli White banned from the sport, and put Jones, Bonds, Giambi, and Romanowski under suspicion from their sports' governing bodies. Greg Anderson, along with Conte, is currently under indictment for trafficking in anabolic steroids.

There have been many, many more incidents of anabolic steroid and other performance-enhancing drug use in the history of sport. Some may eventually be known; others will remain hidden forever. In the past, individuals and nations were motivated by glory. Now money, in terms of salaries and endorsement contracts, is the prime motivator.

Trying to recount the history of performance-enhancing substances and other doping in sport and in society is similar to standing on the bow of the *Titanic* and trying to describe the iceberg. You can't see all of it because so much is hidden, but you still know enough to turn.

4

How Steroids Work,
and What They Do to the Body

IN WHATEVER FORM it is taken (oral, injected, transdermal patch, sublingual liquid, or ointment/gel), an anabolic steroid must first bind with a testosterone receptor in a muscle cell. These receptors exist because the human body produces testosterone naturally. The receptors then stimulate increased production of RNA, which delivers DNA's genetic message to the cytoplasm of a cell where proteins are made. The muscle cells then utilize this increased RNA to produce more protein, which is necessary for strength and muscle mass.

Testosterone, which is the primary active ingredient—in synthetic form—in any anabolic steroid, acts directly in muscle tissue. It increases the speed at which muscle cells are produced and repaired. This same action that stimulates protein synthesis also serves to inhibit protein degradation. This inhibition is known as the anti-catabolic effect (catabolism is a destructive metabolic process by which organisms convert substances into excreted compounds) and plays a major role in allowing the anabolic steroid user to train more often with heavy resistance. The user must also maintain a high-protein and fairly high-calorie diet during the training regimen.

A necessary component in the use of steroids, in order to realize gains in strength, muscle growth, and lean body mass, is heavy resistance training. Because of the anti-catabolic effect, the steroid user does not have to wait forty-eight hours for the muscles to recover from a previous bout of heavy resistance training. Instead of having to work the upper body one day and the lower body the next, the steroid user can work the full body every day with heavy resistance, without having to worry about the effects of muscle breakdown.

A psychological effect also flows from the steroid, possibly from the release of endogenous endorphins. These occur naturally in the body's biochemical compounds, produced by the pituitary gland and the hypothalamus in vertebrates. They resemble the opiates in their abilities to produce analgesia and a sense of well-being, and function as a sort of natural painkiller. They enhance resistance training in that the anabolic steroid user allegedly experiences less fatigue, allowing the lifting of heavy weights during longer workout sessions.

Another psychological effect is the almost compulsive desire of the anabolic steroid user to see results—greater strength, muscle mass, and muscle definition. These are the individuals in the gym or health club who spend an inordinate amount of time looking into the floor-to-ceiling mirrors and flexing to observe the results of their chemically aided workouts.

The anabolic steroid thus functions as an enabler. It permits longer, more frequent, and heavier resistance workouts. Without these workouts the steroids will not produce desired results. Exercise increases the number of testosterone receptor sites in skeletal muscle cells. If one could do the same continous heavy workouts without the use of anabolic steroids (which can't be done because of muscle breakdown), probably nearly all of the same beneficial results could be achieved.

Ben Johnson, the Canadian Olympic sprinter stripped of his gold medal after testing positive for the anabolic steroid Stanozolol at the 1988 Olympic Games in Seoul, did not become a world-record-holding sprinter merely because he used anabolic steroids. Rather, steroids allowed him to do the type of workout that developed his upper- and lower-body muscles to propel him down the track at an extremely rapid rate of speed. He still had to have the proper genetics, still had to work constantly on starts and running form, and still had to tirelessly practice his skills. Steroids merely gave him the "edge" to do all the other things necessary to achieve the desired results.

THE EFFECTS OF STEROIDS

In order to understand the effects of anabolic steroids and other performance-enhancing drugs on the normal function of the human body, it's necessary to understand how certain organs of the body work. The adverse physiological and psychological side effects described here are not intended to frighten the reader but simply to point out possible effects and side effects.

Many androgenic-anabolic steroid (AAS) users take doses that far exceed any therapeutic level. The amount of dosage and the length of time over which the substance is taken are major determinants of the extent of possible side effects. Because of the secrecy that has surrounded AAS usage, there have been very few long-term studies on users. Not everyone who uses these substances will suffer a disease or condition. But, as in the lottery, the odds are good when you win but very bad when you get the condition you thought was a 1000-to-1 chance.

The liver is the largest internal organ of the body. It acts as a major defense mechanism against ingested substances that are potentially harmful to the body, including steroids, and against by-products of metabolism that may become toxic if they are allowed to accumulate, including those produced by steroids. The liver detoxifies these substances by altering their chemical and physical properties to make them less toxic and/or easier for the body to eliminate. The usual example of this process is the conversion of ammonia (a by-product of amino acid metabolism) to urea. Ammonia is toxic to the human body and not easily removed from circulation by the kidneys. Urea, however, is much less toxic and easily eliminated by the kidneys in the form of urine.

The common diseases that attack the liver are cirrhosis, jaundice, and hepatitis, but it's the various forms of hepatitis that are of most concern to us. Since most steroid users inject the drug, unsanitary needles are common. The sharing of hypodermic needles and other drug paraphernalia can transmit Hepatitis B.

Hepatitis B is a serious disease caused by a virus that attacks the liver. The virus can cause lifelong infection, cirrhosis (scarring) of the liver, liver cancer, liver failure, and death. Athletic and other health-care providers should be vaccinated against Hepatitis B because it can be transmitted when blood or bodily fluids from an infected person enter the body of a nonimmune person.

Hepatitis D needs the Hepatitis B virus to exist. It is acquired as a co-infection of Hepatitis B. Often co-infection patients become candidates for liver transplant.

Hepatitis C results in a chronic (long-lasting) infection for up to 85 percent of those infected and chronic liver disease for up to 70 percent of those chronically infected. Transmission commonly occurs when the blood or bodily fluid of an infected individual enters the body of a person who is not infected. Hepatitis C may be transmitted through the sharing of hypodermic needles or syringes when injecting drugs.

Anabolic steroids themselves may damage the liver, especially if they are taken orally. Injectable anabolic steroids, such as testosterone cypionate and testosterone enanthate, seem to have little adverse effect on the liver. But lesions of the liver have been reported after injection of nortestosterone and also occasionally after injection of testosterone esters.

Because of the secrecy involved in the use of anabolic steroids for performance enhancement, the influence of anabolic steroids on liver function has been studied extensively only among hospitalized patients who have been treated for prolonged periods for various diseases such as anemia, renal insufficiency, impotence, and dysfunction of the pituitary gland. In clinical trials, treatment with anabolic steroids has resulted in a reduced excretion of bile from the liver. When little or no bile is secreted, or the flow of bile into the digestive tract is obstructed, itch and jaundice may appear. The condition may also lead to hypertension or fatal bleeding.

There are rather strong indications that tumors of the liver, both benign and malignant, are caused when the anabolic steroids contain a 17-alpha-alkyl group. Usually the tumors are benign adenomas that reverse after stopping the use of steroids. But there are some indications that the use of anabolic steroids by athletes may lead to liver cancer.

Anabolic steroid use is often associated with an increase in plasma activity of liver enzymes, which reflects damage to the organ. Individuals with abnormal liver function appear to be most at risk for this sort of damage.

One of the most serious possible side effects of anabolic steroids (primarily with the use of oral steroids such as Dianabol and Winstrol) is hepatic peliosis. This is the development of bleeding, swelling, and cysts in the liver, a malignant disease with symptoms that include loss of appetite, weakness, bloating, jaundice, and upper abdominal discomfort.

The cardiovascular system, made up of the heart, the blood, and blood vessels, may also suffer damage as a result of the use of anabolic steroids. Blood coursing from the heart delivers oxygen and nutrients to every part of the body. On the return trip, the blood picks up waste products so that the human body can get rid of them.

The human heart is a muscle that actually acts as two pumps in one. The right side of the heart receives blood from the body and pumps it through pulmonary circulation to the lungs, returning it to the left side of the heart. The left side of the heart pumps blood through the circulatory system, which delivers oxygen and nutrients to body tissues and collects carbon dioxide and other waste products which are then carried back through the veins to the right side of the heart, where the process begins all over again.

This flow of blood through the body is determined by cardiac output, which depends on such factors as heart rate (the number of contractions or beats per minute), stroke volume (the amount of blood pumped into the arteries by each contraction), and minute volume (the amount of blood pumped into the arteries in one minute). Blood flow declines when blood vessels narrow and resistance increases, and improves substantially when blood vessel diameter increases.

The heart of a healthy, average-sized human pumps approximately 1,900 gallons of blood each day. During vigorous exercise, the amount of blood pumped per minute increases several fold as compared to the heart at rest. For exercise purposes, the maximal heart rate for an individual is calculated by subtracting the individual's age from 220. In other words, the maximal exercise heart rate for a 30-year-old would be 190. Then, a percentage of that maximal heart rate is used to determine the individual's training heart rate. For a highly trained aerobic athlete, this percentage may be upward of 75 percent of the maximal heart rate. For an average individual, the training heart rate level would be set substantially lower.

Blood pressure is the force of blood exerted on the inside walls of blood vessels. Blood pressure is expressed as a ratio (example: 120/80, read as "120 over 80"). The first number is the systolic pressure, or the pressure when the heart pushes blood out into the arteries. The second number is the diastolic pressure, or the pressure when the heart rests. The heart is a pump. If the blood pressure is elevated, especially in the diastolic reading, that means that the pump is not getting enough rest, is essentially working constantly, and is therefore subject to damage or failure.

No long-term studies have been conducted into the effects of anabolic steroids on the heart and the vascular system. Again, this is due to the secrecy surrounding the use of anabolic steroids. Some evidence from short-term studies suggests that anabolic steroids may cause structural changes to the heart, and that heart disease and strokes are possible, especially with oral usage.

Four main cardiac risk factors are out of our control: heredity, ethnicity, gender, and age. But the seven cardiac risk factors that are controllable—tobacco use, cholesterol, blood pressure, physical condition, obesity, stress, and substance abuse—may be complicated by steroid use.

High blood cholesterol is a risk factor that can definitely be adversely affected by the use of anabolic steroids because of their effect on both HDL (high-density lipoproteins) and LDL (low-density lipoproteins). This is especially true of oral anabolic steroid users, who exhibit both a decline in HDL (good cholesterol) and an increase in LDL (bad cholesterol). Blood levels of HDL, LDL, and triglycerides gradually return to normal after anabolic steroid usage is stopped. But continuous use maintains blood conditions that could cause atherosclerosis (a hardening of the arteries) and lead to heart attack or stroke.

Some data suggest that high doses of anabolic steroids increase diastolic blood pressure. Such increases normalize within six to eight weeks after discontinuing use. It appears that repeated intermittent use of anabolic steroids does not affect diastolic blood pressure during drug-free periods.

Body mass and the ratio of LDL to HDL cholesterol—both factors of anabolic steroid usage—will have a definite adverse effect on blood pressure. The greater the mass of an individual (the average NFL offensive lineman weighs over 320 pounds), the more work the heart is required to do. And if LDL adheres to the wall of a blood vessel, it will decrease the flow of blood through that vessel and force the heart to work harder. Meanwhile the reduction in HDL (which acts to prevent this buildup in the blood vessels) has been found to be caused by the stimulation of a liver enzyme, another product of steroid use.

It should be noted that individuals who used only injectable anabolic steroids did not exhibit this HDL reduction. But most individuals who use injectable anabolic steroids do so in combination with the use of oral varieties.

Another cardiac condition associated with the use of anabolic steroids that deserves mention here is enlargement of the heart beyond that level resulting from exercise alone. As the heart enlarges, its pumping slows—it pumps harder but less. Probably the most famous case of an enlarged heart and reduced cardiac output is that of Steve Courson, an offensive lineman with the Pittsburgh Steelers' NFL championship teams of the late 1970s. Courson, who admittedly used both oral and injectable anabolic steroids for more than fifteen years while playing football in college and the pros, developed an enlarged left ventricle and subsequently was placed on a waiting list for a heart transplant. Fortunately Courson lost weight (approximately eighty pounds) and through medical treatment, diet, and exercise has made an astounding recovery.

Another cardiovascular risk for steroid users is thrombic stroke, a type of stroke due to loss of blood flow to a portion of the brain. It results when a coronary artery is blocked by a blood clot that forms on the plaque in that artery.

Anabolic steroid users run the spectrum from athletes to body builders, police officers, corporate executives, stockbrokers, students, and many, many other life situations. Everyone experiences some distress in their lives, but the anabolic steroid user has at least one more stressor: he or she is using an illegal substance. What's more, anabolic steroid users are often faced with unwanted physical side effects because they are not being medically monitored by a physician. You can only imagine, for example, the stress that might be caused by shrunken testicles.

Anabolic steroids were originally developed to treat medical conditions such as hypogonadism, pathologically delayed puberty, metastatic breast cancer, and the severe muscle wasting of AIDS patients. Any use other than these constitutes substance abuse, plain and simple. Individuals who use anabolic steroids for their performance-enhancing properties normally take significantly higher dosages for periods far exceeding therapeutic parameters.

Because the kidneys are involved in the filtration and removal of metabolic by-products from the body, they may be affected by the use of anabolic steroids. Kidney damage is most likely to appear when the anabolic steroid user is suffering from elevated blood pressure, which will stress the kidneys. Some evidence suggests that anabolic steroid use may be linked to the onset of cancerous tumors in the kidneys of adults, a rapidly growing type normally seen in children and infants. The kidneys are vital to one's heath, so the possibility of any kind of damage should not be ignored during anabolic steroid usage.

If the user notices a darkening of the urine—in some cases a distinguishable amount of blood—or difficulty when urinating, kidney stress may be a legitimate possibility. Other warning signs include pain in the lower back (particularly in the kidney area), fever, and swelling.

The musculoskeletal system may also be damaged by long-term, high-dosage anabolic steroid usage. The primary areas at risk for serious injury are the tendons and ligaments. In the absence of significant scientific studies, two prevalent theories would appear to have scientific merit. The first theory suggests that while using androgenic-anabolic steroids, the muscles grow at a fairly rapid rate while the tendons and ligaments (connective rather than muscle tissue) remain unaffected. Therefore the muscles overpower the tendons and ligaments, causing tears in the tissue.

The second theory relates to psychological and physiological factors involved with androgenic-anabolic steroid usage. Because the breakdown of bodily proteins for energy and raw materials is minimized by the use of androgenic-anabolic steroids, recovery time after a heavy resistance workout is shortened, allowing the individual to get back into the weight room sooner and work a greater spectrum of muscles on a regular basis. Normally, without androgenic-anabolic steroids, an individual could do a complete body workout only every forty-eight hours, allowing time for the body to recover. With the aid of steroids, the individual can do a full body workout every day. Tendons and ligaments (even muscles) are thus subjected to wear-and-tear injuries from these virtually perpetual workouts. Over time, through repetition, this microtrauma breaks a threshold and injury occurs. It is simply a case of overworking these structures to the point where minor injuries add up to a major injury. The musculoskeletal structure is pushed beyond its yield point and fails.

The adverse side effects of androgenic-anabolic steroids on adolescents can be devastating because of the possibility of stunted growth. There are no significant scientific studies of steroid use in adolescents. Given the growth in steroid abuse among this important population, the chance that we may see new or more significant effects is especially worrisome.

SOME STUDIES in the former Communist sports machines of Soviet Russia and their satellites, especially East Germany, are chilling in their findings. In effect these countries used their athletes as guinea pigs for experimentation, hoping that winning medals and setting records would offset any damage. A landmark study of Soviet weightlifters in 1952 revealed that many of them had to use urinary catheters. It is highly probable that this was necessitated by the enlargement of their prostate glands caused by the androgenic-anabolic steroids they were using.

Some members of the scientific community have argued that short-term, low-dosage anabolic steroid usage by males may not produce dramatic or long-term physiological damage. The problem with this thinking is that anabolic steroid usage is seldom low dosage or short term. For females, who have a lower level of testosterone occurring naturally in the body, the physiological effects of anabolic steroids tend to be more profound and often irreversible.

THE ADVERSE psychological side effects suffered by some anabolic steroid users can be even more disastrous than the physiological problems, because the sufferers are less likely to seek early treatment. First and foremost among the potentially dangerous psychological side effects is addiction. While no accepted scientific study has concluded that anabolic steroid use is physiologically addictive, numerous such studies have concluded that it is psychologically addictive.

An addiction may be positive or negative. Exercising on a daily basis can be a very positive addiction because of its physiological benefits and the pleasure it brings to the exerciser who feels better and looks better. But if this exercise addiction becomes obsessive-compulsive, it can be transformed into a negative addiction. Most athletes love to compete in a game or match but frankly dread the drudgery of daily practices or workouts necessary to maintain or improve their competitive level. Why do they subject themselves to this often boring and painful practice routine?

Because they enjoy the games or matches so much. They are addicted to the psychological high they experience in competition.

Most all of us have an innate desire to experience pleasure. Those individuals who are willing to persist through boredom and pain to experience that pleasure over a prolonged period of time are exhibiting an addictive personality. In the course of my travels I have seen forty-year-old men competing in extremely volatile "flag football" leagues in the parks of Chicago. They are not paid to compete. Their feats will not be reported in the *Chicago Tribune*. They do it because of the addictive "high" they experience from the competition. In St. Petersburg, Florida, you can find a baseball league with a minimum age of sixty-five for participants; they play a sixty-game schedule.

This is by no means a purely American phenomenon. While traveling in Asia and Central America I observed fifty- and sixty-year-olds playing a relatively high level of league soccer. In Canada it is not uncommon to find ice hockey leagues with players well into their sixties. The pleasure-seeking principle keeps these individuals participating. But when this thirst for competition becomes compulsive behavior, beyond the level of reasonableness, it becomes a negative addiction.

Anabolic steroid users are fair game for negative addiction and other psychological side effects of illegal drug usage. Anyone who exercises will eventually reach a plateau beyond which effort does not produce equivalent results. There is an individual physiological maximum. At that point an individual can either accept this limitation (the psychologically healthy response) or seek other means, such as beginning, continuing, or increasing the usage of anabolic steroids or other substances to reach beyond the inherent physiological limitation (the psychologically unhealthy response).

Some of the adverse psychological side effects of anabolic steroids have been identified: aggressive behavior, mood swings, distorted body image, eating disorders, depression, and suicidal tendencies. Not everyone who uses anabolic steroids will develop these conditions, but the consequences for those individuals who do are often catastrophic. It is far too simplistic to call this "roid rage." Anecdotal studies have indicated that individuals on high-dosage anabolic steroids have exhibited heightened irritability and even violent behavior patterns. Some of this behavior manifests itself in temper tantrums, altercations with teammates and opponents, destruction of property (one nineteen-year-old college football player became angry while lifting weights and proceeded to toss hundred-pound weight plates, breaking all the floor-to-ceiling mirrors in the weight room; he then moved on to the student union, where he attacked a security guard before being subdued by five policemen), spousal/partner physical abuse, and murder. One of the more tragic cases involved three-time former Mr. Universe, Bertil Fox, known professionally as the "Mozart of Muscles," who was convicted of murdering his girlfriend and her mother on the island of St. Kitts during a jealous rage while allegedly under the influence of anabolic steroids.

Mood swings related to anabolic steroid usage were studied by use of a retrospective study reported in 1997 in the *Journal of Forensic Psychiatry*. The conclusion of that study, based on court records and police reports, was that anabolic steroids might produce violent behavior and other mental disturbances, including psychoses.

A classic case of such an effect was John Kordic, the ice hockey "tough guy" who used anabolic steroids and cocaine. On the night of August 8, 1992, Kordic fought with nine Royal Canadian Mounted Policemen at Quebec's Motel Maxim. The Mounties eventually subdued him, needing two pairs of handcuffs to restrain his arms. Kordic died on the way to the hospital.

Another professional hockey player alleged to be an anabolic steroid user, Mike Danton, tried in 2004 to hire an assassin to kill his agent because his paranoia led him to believe that the agent had hired someone to kill him. Fortunately no one was killed, but Danton and a co-conspirator were tried for conspiracy to murder the agent.

Distorted body image can be a significant problem among anabolic steroid users. Some psychologists refer to the phenomenon of the "Lying Mirror": anabolic steroid users can gain great mass and strength, but when they look in the mirror they don't see sufficient results to satisfy them. The vintage ads for Charles Atlas's bodybuilding courses pictured the proverbial "ninety-seven-pound weakling" having sand kicked in his face by a bully at the beach. Some anabolic steroid users, regardless of the size and strength they've achieved, are afraid of becoming the ninety-seven pound weakling being victimized by stronger foes. So they take more and better anabolic steroids and do Herculean workouts with massive weights. It's not unusual for these individuals to spend more than $100 dollars a day for anabolic steroids alone.

Opposite of this "Lying Mirror" syndrome is the individual whose lean body mass has produced a 5 to 8 percent body fat but who, when he looks in the mirror, sees a fat person. I once did a body-fat analysis on a lovely young female bodybuilder. When I gave her the results (10 percent body fat), she began to cry uncontrollably and confessed that she was ashamed of her body. When one considers that the ideal percentage of body fat for a woman under twenty-five years of age ranges from 16 to 26 percent, it's easy to understand how a distorted body image can affect anyone, with an even greater impact on the anabolic steroid user.

Depression is defined medically as a temporary mental state or a chronic mental disorder characterized by feelings of sadness, loneliness, despair, low self-esteem, and self-reproach. If one considers the level of secrecy involved in using an illegal substance, the fear of getting caught, the extent of workouts necessary to maintain the steroid-enhanced body, and the fear of physiological or psychological damage, it is not difficult to understand why anabolic steroid users may experience clinical depression.

Suicidal tendencies and even suicides have been documented. Although some will argue that there have been no documented suicides by high-profile anabolic steroid users, often the cause of death in suicide cases is limited to the direct instrumentality that precipitated the death (gunshot wound, carbon monoxide poisoning, etc.). Elevated testosterone in such cases may not be assessed. Untreated, some depressive symptoms associated with anabolic steroid withdrawal have been known to persist for a year or more after the abuser stops taking the drugs.

ANABOLIC STEROID RESEARCH

Minimal research has been done on anabolic steroids. Further, much of the research has involved populations taking steroids for pathological reasons, such as hypogonadism or AIDS, rather than a healthy, athletic population. Several of these studies involved a relatively low number of subjects, which would clearly affect the validity of the study. Several studies involved questionnaires. Because of the secrecy involved in the use of anabolic agents, and the fact that since 1992 anabolic steroids are classified as a controlled substance, with both possession and distribution subject to felony penalties, individuals are likely to be less than candid about their use, thus rendering questionnaires of minimal value.

One study worth noting is that by Hartgens in 2000, which concluded that eight weeks of self-administered anabolic steroids increased body weight, lean body mass, and limb circumferences, and reduced fat percentage compared with controls. Changes remained six weeks after drug withdrawal, though for some measurements only partially. Anabolic steroids stimulated the bone-free lean mass of all body parts, but it did not affect fat mass.

In light of available research, one may conclude that activities involving mass and strength would be enhanced short term by the use of anabolic agents. There is little question that the use of steroids, combined with a high-protein diet and heavy resistance exercise, will produce greater muscle mass and strength. Thus, bodybuilders, weight lifters, shot-putters, and football linemen could very possibly enhance their performance with the short-term use of anabolic steroids in high dosage. But anabolic steroid use and heavy resistance training alone do not necessarily equal success.

In the summer of 2004, Brock Lesnar, a giant of a man at 295 pounds, former NCAA wrestling champion and professional wrestler, was invited to the Pittsburgh Steelers pre-season Training Camp. There was no question about the man's strength, but his football abilities were an unknown. As it turned out, strength alone was insufficient to overcome his lack of football skills, and Lesnar was eventually cut from the training-camp roster.

Weight lifting, at competitive levels, also requires more than brute strength. A great degree of biomechanics and coordination is involved in making the requisite lifts with heavy weights. So, again, a steroid-enhanced body would be a benefit but no guarantee of success.

The average Olympic shot-putter today weighs approximately three hundred pounds. Sometimes, watching these individuals, it is easy to forget how much athletic prowess is necessary to traverse the ring, biomechanically shift power and energy from the legs, perform the correct pivot with the hip, and keep the body under the shot in order to correctly explode that energy into the put to achieve distances of seventy feet or more. The technique involves the transfer of linear energy to angular energy. Would a steroid-enhanced body help such an individual? Yes, but only if he or she had the necessary athletic talent in the first place.

Bodybuilding is an end-product sport. The actual competition is only a display of what has been accomplished in training sessions. The ability to train heavier and longer without having to experience the catabolic effect is a great advantage, and that's why so many bodybuilders, including the present governor of California, have used anabolic steroids.

It's a credit to the International Federation of Bodybuilding and Fitness (IFBF), developed by Ben and Joe Weider, that they have tried very hard to keep the sport clean and initiated drug testing as part of the founding of the organization. The IFBF follows the International Olympic Committee (IOC) and World Anti-Doping Agency (WADA) guidelines with respect to doping controls. But like any sport that has become more financially rewarding, many bodybuilders are willing to risk using steroids in order to reap the financial rewards that a championship may bring. Similarly, some competitors use designer or less detectable drugs and masking agents that can be found in other, more highly visible sports.

Other than weight throwers, track and field athletes have bettered their performance by using anabolic steroids to strengthen those muscles necessary for their event. Valery Borzov, Olympic gold medalist in 1972 in the one hundred and two hundred meters, was the first "engineered sprinter" developed by Soviet sports science. Officials monitored his diet, developed scientific workouts under the watchful eyes of the coaches, and did whatever else was necessary to produce an Olympic champion and holder of the coveted title of "fastest man in the world." Since this development occurred at the height of the cold war, and since the Russians had been experimenting with the use of anabolic steroids for thirty years, it is not a stretch to conjecture that Borzov's efforts were steroid enhanced. The American Tim Montgomery and the Brit Dwaine Chambers received suspensions for suspected steroid use, which prevented them from competing in the 2004 Olympics.

Sprinting is a sport of form and power. The more strength in the legs, arms, and shoulders that a sprinter can combine with proper mechanics for starting and sprinting, the greater the individual's chances, not only to win the race but to challenge the world record. Since the sprint events are highly visible, the day of the "true amateur" in the sport is a legal myth at best. Talented, successful sprinters receive endorsements, training "subsidies," appearance monies, and financial rewards for winning events. If you "follow the money," it's relatively easy to find the athlete's motivation for gaining the "edge" necessary to reap the rewards, regardless of the ethics and rules of the sport.

For a long time boxing has not been immune to drug problems, including the use of anabolic steroids. Although it is an extremely scientific sport, combining footwork, strategy, hand speed, and hand-and-eye coordination, some boxers have taken the anabolic steroid "shortcut" in an effort to gain strength and lean body mass. After the infamous "Bad Blood" match between Oscar de la Hoya and Fernando Vargas, the Nevada Athletic Commission reported that Vargas had failed his post-fight drug test, testing positive for stanozolol (the same anabolic steroid that cost Ben Johnson his Olympic gold medal when found in his post-victory drug test). Vargas claimed that he had no knowledge of any illegal "supplementation" in his preparation for the bout with de la Hoya, contending that he took only the supplements supplied to him by his handlers.

If Vargas was telling the truth, the incident represents one of the most tragic moral and ethical violations in sport. If athletes, or anyone else for that matter, choose to risk using a banned substance, they are solely to blame for whatever may happen to them. But, as in documented cases of East German and Chinese swimmers, when someone else, particularly someone in a position of trust, violates that trust by causing the athlete unknowingly to use an illegal and potentially harmful substance, that is not only the antithesis of the true spirit of sport, but—as the German courts decided in 1998 in the case of the East German swimmers—"willful infliction of bodily harm" and criminally actionable. This is an important lesson to remember, given the grand jury testimony of

Barry Bonds, who claims that he was given substances that he only later learned contained THG and testosterone.

Probably one of the saddest drug-related boxing stories is that of Bob Hazleton, a promising heavyweight contender in the 1970s who, after losing to George Foreman, decided he needed to bulk up to have any success in the heavyweight class. He chose anabolic steroids and gained twenty-seven pounds. Although the added weight helped him compete and win at the heavyweight level, those victories came with a high price tag. Hazleton began experiencing numbness in his legs, later diagnosed by physicians as anabolic steroid–related blood clots. Even though he discontinued the use of steroids, the damage was already done. Hazleton eventually had to have both his legs amputated.

Although the world of professional boxing has had its problems, it has also had its heroes. A shining example is Roy Jones, Jr., whom I had the honor (along with my colleague Dr. Jon Lim) of working with in 1993 when Jones first considered moving up to the heavyweight classification because he had essentially run out of competition at the light-heavyweight level. Jones, who has never used an illegal substance in his life, is a true natural athlete with the heart of a champion.

Although he was not in training for a fight at the time, Jones completed the treadmill test at a level usually achieved only by elite distance runners. He had an outstanding recovery heart rate. Underwater weight evaluation indicated 6 percent body fat, a figure that would be found in an extremely small number of athletes, regardless of the sport. A role model who realizes his responsibility in that regard, Jones is the greatest pound-for-pound boxer of his era.

Wrestling, as an amateur sport, has also had problems with the use of anabolic steroids and other illegal substances. One of the causes is the need to "make weight" in order to compete at a given weight classification. If a wrestler has the requisite skills, it is clearly a perceived advantage to have added strength and lean mass. Anabolic steroids enable the wrestler to do heavy resistance exercise (again, the anti-catabolic factor) and still have the stamina to practice at a high rate of effort.

Clenbuterol is often abused by wrestlers to help them gain strength and control weight. This is a banned drug used by athletes in power-related and even in endurance sports. The chemical is attractive to athletes because it appears to have an anabolic effect on human muscles, and it may also increase fat metabolism, the so-called thermogenic (fat-burning) effect.

WHO IS MOST AT RISK FOR ADVERSE SIDE EFFECTS?

Other than the leaked secret grand jury testimony, I have no information whether Barry Bonds has used anabolic steroids or any other illegal substance. I hope he hasn't, but if he has, he is an adult with the requisite intelligence to make his own informed decisions. I'm sure he understands the potential consequences. He also possesses—if in fact he has used these substances—the ability and the means to be routinely monitored for liver function and other physiological functions in order to be relatively certain that his body is not damaged by the substances.

I have had several discussions with members of the medical profession regarding the ethics of monitoring someone who is taking a drug for other than the treatment of a pathology, a drug that the physician has not prescribed to the patient. Since there is no legal duty to inform anyone (law enforcement, sport governing bodies, etc.), it would seem that physician-patient confidentiality would apply. Since the physician's duty is to provide the best possible medical care for his patient, it is my position, and that of many of the medical practitioners with whom I have discussed the issue, that it would be medically ethical for the physician to monitor the patient's health status.

There is, however, something of a grey area when it comes to team physicians. Since they are in the team's employ while treating the athletes who come under their care, they have a dual duty. The ignominious new practice of awarding the right to function as team physician to the highest bidder raises new questions. The physician is serving two masters. At some point in the near future, I expect that many athletes or perhaps their agents will employ doctors to treat the athletes outside the traditional team-physician model.

The individual most at risk for adverse side effects from anabolic steroid usage is the person who is not medically monitored. Because of the secrecy that surrounds anabolic steroid usage, those most at risk would seem to be teenage users who might lack the funds for adequate, regular medical monitoring, or whose parents are not aware that their child is using anabolic steroids. Also at greatest risk are those totally uninformed or misinformed individuals who are getting their steroid advice from the biggest person in the weight room or from similarly uninformed or misinformed teammates or associates.

According to the best medical experts I have found, if an individual is taking anabolic steroids at a dosage greater than a therapeutic dose, the following blood tests should be regularly performed:

Alanine transaminase (AST)
Alkaline phosphatase (ALP)
Aspartate Aminotransferase (AST)
Gamma-glutamyl transpeptidase (GGT)
Promthrombin time (PT)
Serum bilirubin

These tests are the components of a Liver Function Panel. The approximate charge for the panel is $185, but charges may vary by location.

To be safe, the anabolic steroid user should have the Liver Function Panel test performed at least every three months, preferably every two months. So the approximate costs per year would range from $740 to $1,100. If these tests were being performed only to monitor anabolic steroid usage, and the individual had no other active pathology to warrant the test, medical insurance would probably not cover the costs.

OTHER PERFORMANCE-ENHANCING SUBSTANCES

Human growth hormone (HGH) and erythropoietin (EPO) occur naturally in the human body, but, like testosterone, both have been artificially bioengineered.

HGH is secreted in the human body by the anterior pituitary gland. Its normal function is to aid the transfer of amino acids across cell membranes that enhance the protein synthesis of the cell. Human growth hormone also plays an important role in maintaining blood glucose levels, helping the uptake of glucose and amino acid in muscle cells, and releasing fatty acids from fat cells. Historically, HGH has been used to treat growth disorders in children and low levels of growth hormone occurring naturally in adults.

Before 1984 the only source of HGH for treatment purposes was an injectable form harvested from the anterior pituitary glands of cadavers. This practice was discontinued in 1984 upon the discovery that it was positively linked with the development in injected persons of Creutzfeldt-Jakob disease, a rare and fatal brain disorder, better known as "mad cow disease."

In 1985 the pharmaceutical company Genentech successfully developed the biopharmaceutical Protropin, essentially a synthesized human growth hormone, for the specific purpose of treating children with this hormone deficiency. As is often the case, any drug that can be used can also be abused. There is some evidence that cadaver-harvested HGH was injected into young female East German swimmers in the late 1970s. Genetically engineered HGH is one of the drugs allegedly confessed to being used by Jason Giambi of the New York Yankees during his "secret" grand jury testimony regarding the BALCO investigation. It has been a documented favorite of bodybuilders for the past twenty years because of the way it promotes muscle growth through protein synthesis, and burns fat.

Although HGH has been banned by virtually every sports governing authority, historically it has been difficult to detect because it occurs naturally in the human body. It is rumored that sectors of the athletic community dubbed the 1996 Olympics in Atlanta the "HGH Celebration Games." Recently blood tests have been developed for the detection of unusually high levels of HGH. While this may seem to be the answer to detecting the hormone, one must remember that many sports governing bodies, including the recently developed Major League Baseball Drug Testing Policy, do not have the authority to require blood samples for drug-detection purposes.

Adverse side effects possible from the use of HGH are those associated with acromegaly, a chronic metabolic disorder caused by the presence of too much growth hormone. It results in gradual enlargement of body tissues, including the bones of the face, jaw, hands, feet, and skull. The late Andre Rene Roussimoff, known professionally as the wrestler "Andre the Giant," was a classic example of pathological acromegaly. He stood seven feet four inches tall and weighed over five hundred pounds. Like many of those who have this condition, Roussimoff died at the relatively tender age of forty-seven.

Another possible side effect of the use of HGH, when there is no deficiency of natural HGH in the body, is that the body's homeostatic regulator may signal the anterior pituitary gland to cease production of the hormone. Should this occur, it is probably a permanent cessation, and the individual will have to depend on genetically engineered HGH for the remainder of his or her life.

Athletes are not the only individuals who abuse HGH. Hundreds of "fountain of youth" clinics provide (for an extremely high fee) HGH to "patients" who want to ward off signs of aging—as slower metabolism, wrinkles, and skin problems. These "vanity clients" are willing to risk virtually anything in an attempt to maintain or regain their youthful appearance.

Erythropoietin (EPO) is a naturally occurring glycoprotein hormone that plays a primary role in the process of red-blood-cell production, which normally occurs in the blood-forming tissue of the bone marrow. This hormone is produced by specialized cells in the kidneys that are sensitive to oxygen concentration in the blood. If the oxygen concentration is too low, these cells increase the release of EPO. Since oxygen is carried by the red blood cells, too few red blood cells (anemia) will also signal the release of EPO. EPO acts on stem cells in the bone marrow to increase the production of red blood cells. Because red blood cells carry oxygen to the muscles, and because endurance athletes need a huge amount of oxygen during their arduous sport, raising the number of red blood cells can—theoretically—improve performance.

Before the development of recombinant EPO, or rEPO, endurance athletes tried to increase the number of red blood cells by removing their own blood at the height of their training program, storing it while they went through their pre-event taper, and transfusing it back just before the event. Testing and timing were the keys to this autologous blood-doping. One had to determine the zenith of preparation and capture the blood with the greatest number of oxygen-carrying red blood cells, then transfuse the blood back into the bloodstream as close as possible to the time of competition. A former colleague, Dr. Tom LaBlonde, reported to me that in 1976, when he was invited to observe the Eastern-bloc sports medicine programs, there was so much blood being taken and transfused that the sports medicine labs looked more like Red Cross blood banks.

Since EPO is a naturally occurring hormone, testing for it is virtually impossible. Unable to measure EPO itself, the governing bodies of international sport at first relied on a surrogate test that measured the density of cells in the blood. Blood is composed of cells—mainly red, but also white—along with serum and other liquids that help the cells flow. A study from the 1980s, before the availability of recombinant EPO, showed that endurance athletes' blood averaged a cellular content of 43 percent, so the governing bodies determined that any athlete with a level above 50 percent would be disqualified for blood doping.

Then technology came to the aid of blood dopers. Amgen, a biotechnology company, first filed a patent application on the cloning of the recombinant EPO gene in late 1983, and three years later obtained its first patent on EPO. Amgen subsequently marketed its product under the brand name Epogen, a recombinant form of EPO produced using ovary cells isolated from the Chinese hamster. This product was originally intended for the treatment of anemia and as an aid to dialysis patients. But it did not take long for rEPO to get into the hands—or rather the veins—of endurance athletes. Instead of having to collect and reinfuse blood, the endurance athlete needed only to receive an intravenous or subcutaneous injection of rEPO within twenty-four hours of the endurance event in which he or she was competing. Now the only true way of testing for rEPO doping is by measuring the hematocrit of the athlete. If that hematocrit is elevated, it is a suspicion of blood doping—but not medically reliable evidence because of the variation in hematocrit levels among individuals naturally. To date, despite the protests of several regulatory boards, there is no accepted and definitive test for rEPO doping.

The benefits accruing to the endurance athlete user of rEPO would include the greater oxygen-carrying capacity of red blood cells, more oxygen in the blood because of more red blood cells, and more time before exhaustion. It is rEPO that Tour de France cyclists turn to for that extra boost.

Since the human body produces EPO naturally, when rEPO is injected into a healthy body, the body may stop producing EPO on its own or produce a smaller amount. This usually returns to normal levels after rEPO use is discontinued. Another side effect of rEPO administration is that the blood may become viscous (thick) because of the relationship of the number of red blood cells to plasma volume. In the worst-case scenario, this thickened blood could cause clots to form in the circulatory system, possibly causing stroke or heart attack. Again, these side effects have been rare, but the risk would seem an awfully high price to pay for enhanced performance.

The effects, both intended and unintended, of anabolic steroids and other doping agents are significant. Yes, many of the drugs we have described have valid, positive medical uses, and there is no reason to place further controls or limits on their proper use. An argument may even be made for something approaching legalization for some of these drugs. Proper medical supervision, including testing for such things as blood levels and liver function, could reduce medical problems and perhaps open a line of communication between doctor and patient that might stop the misuse of these drugs. But as athletes turn to these drugs on their own, seeking an advantage, they play a chemical roulette with their health and well-being. Simply put, none of these drugs would meet any scientific standard of safety for use by athletes.

The first weapon in any battle is knowledge. Consider yourself armed.

5

The Original Juice:
Amphetamines and Uppers

AMPHETAMINES are a group of synthetic psychoactive drugs that stimulate both the central nervous system and the sympathetic division of the peripheral nervous system. The collective group of amphetamines includes amphetamine, dextroamphetamine, and methamphetamine. The drug can be traced back to a German chemist named Edeleano, who synthesized it in 1887 and did not recognize its stimulant effects. Its original name was phenylisopropylamine, and it had no purpose or medical use.

In the early 1930s, when amphetamine's properties for stimulating the central nervous system and its use as a respiratory stimulant were discovered, it was marketed as an inhaler for nasal congestion under the brand name Benzedrine. Medical professionals recommended it as a cure for a range of ailments—alcohol hangover, narcolepsy, depression, weight reduction, hyperactivity in children, and vomiting associated with pregnancy.

The use of amphetamine grew rapidly because it was inexpensive, readily available, had long-lasting effects, and seemingly did not pose a risk of addiction. Oral and intravenous preparations of amphetamine derivatives, including methamphetamine, were developed and became available for therapeutic purposes. During World War II the military in the United States, Great Britain, Germany, and Japan used amphetamines to increase alertness and endurance and to improve the mood of their soldiers.

In the United States in the 1950s, legally manufactured tablets of both dextroamphetamine (Dexedrine) and methamphetamine (Methedrine) became readily available and were used nonmedically by college students, truck drivers, and athletes. As their use spread, so did their abuse. Amphetamines became a cure-all for such things as weight control and the treatment of mild depression. This pattern changed drastically in the 1960s with the increased availability of injectable methamphetamine. The 1970 Controlled Substances Act severely restricted the legal production of injectable methamphetamine.

The medical use of amphetamines is now limited, with only Dexedrine currently available for use in the treatment of narcolepsy, a rare condition where the patient cannot help suddenly falling asleep. The only other amphetamine-related drug available for medical use is methylphenidate (Ritalin) for the treatment of attention deficit disorder in children. (Ritalin is not strictly an amphetamine, though it is very similar in chemical structure and effects.)

Amphetamines are absorbed from the small intestine. The peak concentration in the blood occurs in one to two hours following use. Absorption is usually complete in two and a half to four hours and is accelerated by food intake. Amphetamine metabolites are excreted in the urine. The use of these drugs is being further reduced by nonamphetamine alternatives, such as Strattera for ADD and Provigil for narcolepsy. Amphetamine limits appetite, increases body temperature, and has sympathetic effects on cardiovascular and respiratory functions. Amphetamines increase alertness and arousal, but an extended level of arousal may change to anxiety or panic.

Amphetamines have a fairly long history of abuse in sports. They were reportedly used by soccer players, boxers, cyclists, and speed skaters in the 1930s and 1940s, during both training and competition. Professional baseball players returning from World War II brought back tales of how amphetamines had allowed them to stay awake for days at a time and still be alert. By the late 1960s, amphetamines were often openly displayed in jars in major league dressing rooms, and players were known to grab a handful and swallow them before games.

In 1967 the death of the British cyclist Tommy Simpson during the Tour de France shocked the world of sport. Simpson was twenty-nine years old, fit and strong. He was the first Brit to make his mark in the world of European cycling and was adored by the sporting public. They were shocked by the results of the autopsy which indicated amphetamines in Simpson's bloodstream. Amphetamine tablets were also found in the pocket of his race jersey and in his hotel room. According to rumors in the cycling community, Simpson had begun using amphetamines while training in Belgium before the fatal 1967 race.

Why would an athlete want to take amphetamines? In professional sports the accumulation of games and travel has a wearing effect on players. With eighty-one games at home and the same number on the road, not to mention spring training and the playoffs, it is easy to understand how a baseball player can be worn down. Schedules in professional basketball are just as rough. And every team has some players known as "bad livers" because they like the nightlife and often do not get enough rest at night. Amphetamines often become the magic bullet to make up for a long plane ride or a late night out. Author and player Jim Bouton said,

[75]

"Steroids make you better. Uppers [amphetamines] just make you play up to your potential when you're hung over."

Athletes also turn to amphetamines for "the edge," that special something that will help them perform above their talent level. Athletes or other physically active persons may experience enhanced awareness, better hand-eye coordination, and a sense of greater energy while under the effects of amphetamines.

But for every good thing a performance-enhancing substance has to offer, it always seems to carry serious baggage. Some of the more common side effects of amphetamines are dry mouth, gastrointestinal problems, heart palpitations, elevated blood pressure and rapid heart rate, and possible liver damage. Habitual, repeated use of amphetamines results in amphetamine addiction.

Amphetamines excite the central nervous system. They cause an overall sense of well-being for six to eight hours, followed by agitation that can cause violent behavior. Repeated use increases an individual's tolerance to the drug. As tolerance builds, more of the drug is needed to achieve a desired effect. Classic signs of addiction appear with amphetamine use. When the drug is stopped, withdrawal symptoms may appear.

Not every person, athlete or otherwise, who uses amphetamines will become addicted, but the risk factor is significant. A recent study by the UCLA Medical Center concluded that amphetamines were the largest co-addiction factor (when individuals are physiologically or psychologically addicted to more than one substance) of any of the studied drugs.

The psychological addictive factor of amphetamines is much harder to combat than the physiological factor. Medical science has drugs to help wean people off of other drugs. But it's not a Yogi Berra quote to say that the mind has a mind of its own. Amphetamines can induce exhilarating perceptions of power, strength, energy, focus, and enhanced motivation while diminishing the perceived need for food and sleep. These are all seen as positives by someone whose work involves large outlays of energy, the need to focus (as when a ninety-mile-per-hour fastball is being thrown in your direction), and demanding travel schedules that produce jet lag.

While the psychologically addictive aspects of amphetamine usage are more difficult to deal with, the physiological aspects present a good many everyday problems. Decreased appetite can lead to "walking malnutrition," a condition caused by the failure of the hunger reflex to motivate the individual to eat regularly. Malnutrition and body wasting is readily apparent in "tweakers," users of crystal methamphetamine who will stay awake for days.

Sleeplessness is another issue that eventually causes bodily distress. Adults should have approximately seven hours of restful sleep per night, but amphetamine users will not feel the need for that much sleep (and the aroused state of the body under amphetamine influence will not allow the sleep anyway), so they build up a sleep deficit. This deficit cannot be made up by "crashing" and sleeping for lengthy periods. Instead the body must slowly transition into a correct sleep pattern.

The timing of rest becomes another problem with amphetamine use. If an athlete is on the road, staying in a hotel and playing a night game, the schedule of activities is altered and the "body clock" is disturbed. Humans are creatures of habit, and the body adjusts to those habits. When habits are suddenly changed, as in exercise or sleep patterns, the body clock becomes confused, with adverse mental and physical effects on the individual.

"Power naps" to combat altered schedules are a change in the sleep pattern with potentially damaging effects later. Athletes wake up from a "power nap" and feel drowsy, but they have to perform in four hours. So they reach for an amphetamine (or two or more) to get their bodies charged up for the game. The amphetamine effects will be felt within an hour and may last up to six or eight hours depending on the dosage. Some athletes have been known to take additional amphetamines a half-hour before game time, so that they will be alert throughout the game. After the game, players may grab a late snack and try to get some rest for the next day. But that rest certainly won't come easily because of the combination of elevated heart rate from exercise and the arousal still in effect from the amphetamines. The next morning, feeling basically lousy, they may reach for another amphetamine (or two or more) to get "started." This is how the cycle of abuse and addiction works.

A combination of amphetamines and painkillers, which have almost diametrically opposite effects in the body, further confuses the body's chemistry. The addicted athlete will reach for another type of medication to treat the effects of that confusion, only making the problem worse. Again, the cycle of addiction is brought into play.

Major League Baseball's new drug-testing agreement, signed in late 2004, specifically does not address amphetamines or similar substances. During negotiations it was often a question what the players were getting back for their historic acquiescence in a testing program. Many inside the game think that keeping amphetamines and other uppers off the banned list was the giveback. Players will not be tested for them, and there are no penalties for their use. The owners' chief negotiator, Rob Manfred, said the use of amphetamines was too complex an issue for baseball to address now. "Stimulants are a complicated area," he said. "Are they performance enhancing? How should they be regulated? That's something [we will] look at [in the future] because we weren't prepared to deal with it."

This is another case of Major League Baseball avoiding a real issue for public relations purposes. Amphetamines are just as important a problem as anabolic steroids. Gary Wadler, a board member of the World Anti-Doping Agency and an expert in performance-enhancing drugs as well as a professor of medicine at New York University, has gone on record as saying that research shows amphetamines to be possibly more performance enhancing than anabolic steroids, and that more athletes are using them. He referred to baseball's new drug policy as a "Band-Aid," a cover-up with no healing power. Baseball wants to proclaim to the public, "See, we have solved the steroids problem, so you can keep on coming to the games and spending money."

Former Texas Ranger Chad Curtis told a *Sports Illustrated* writer in 2004, "You might have one team where eight guys play naked [without using amphetamines] and another team where nobody does. . . . Steroids are popular, but quite a lot more guys take [amphetamines] than steroids. I'm talking about illegal stuff. Speed . . . Ritalin, which is legal only with a doctor's prescription . . . sometimes guys don't even know what they're taking. One guy will take some pills out of his locker and tell somebody else, 'Here, take one of these. You'll feel better.' And the other guy will take it and not even know what it is." Curtis added that amphetamine use is so prevalent that nonusers are sometimes ostracized as slackers.

It's time for professional and so-called amateur sports organizations to address amphetamine usage and addiction as a true health issue. For Major League Baseball, the message should be loud and clear: Don't clean up baseball for public relations reasons. Don't clean it up for the fans. Clean up baseball for the game and for the health of its players.

6

Supplements, a Grey Area

SPORTS SUPPLEMENTS are everywhere. They are sold in health-food stores and drugstores, at Wal-Mart, by mail order, and via the internet. Last year it's estimated that Americans alone spent more than $4 billion on sports supplements. And this figure may be somewhat understated because of the difficulty in tracking internet sales.

The Dietary Supplements and Health Education Act of 1994 (DSHEA) is the statutory authority for the regulation of the supplement industry. The DSHEA definition of a dietary supplement is "a product intended to supplement the diet that bears or contains one or more of the following dietary ingredients: vitamin, mineral or amino acid; herb or other botanical; dietary substance; concentrate, metabolite, constituent or combination."

The pre-market safety determination of a dietary supplement is left largely up to the manufacturer of the substance (sort of like letting the fox guard the henhouse). The responsibility of the Food and Drug Administration is to remove unsafe ingredients or products from the market, and to do so it must demonstrate that the product poses a significant or unreasonable risk to the consumer. So when you buy a sports supplement, which is classified as a dietary supplement, your safety in using the product depends on how much due diligence the manufacturer did in terms of nonbiased research before sending the product to market. When it comes to sports supplement manufacturers, there are some very good ones and some very bad ones; most fall somewhere in between.

Profit margins on sports supplements are astronomical. The major costs to the manufacturer are advertising and packaging, because the ingredients are quite inexpensive. But product prices are high. Margins can approach 400 percent. Some college athletes spend more than $1,000 a month on dietary supplements, and bodybuilders spend even more.

People who consider using a dietary supplement should first analyze their food intake. They should keep a dietary diary and determine how they stand versus the recommended daily allowances for active persons. If a normal diet is providing everything they need, supplements aren't necessary. If their diet proves to be deficient in some areas, it may be in their best interest to supplement those deficiencies, especially if they are interested in athletic performance. The recommended diet of an active individual should be approximately 65 percent carbohydrate, 25 percent fat, and 10 percent protein. (Atkins devotees have our condolences.)

It's often difficult to determine from the label of a supplement exactly what it contains and in what proportions. Some of the ingredients are listed as proprietary (protected by trademark or patent); other ingredients are not necessarily listed in descending order of percentage amount.

Consumers should read the label of the supplement for the ingredients and the manufacturer's claims—such as "builds strong muscles"—but also research these ingredients. Does the consumer need them, and if so in what quantity? Diet should be examined to see if there are true deficiencies in the recommended daily allowance (RDA or RV) of each of the ingredients in the supplement. This is not to say that RDA should be the only determinant. Obviously if people are exercising vigorously, they will expend more energy than those who are less active. But RDA should be used as a point of reference.

The bottom line is that supplement shopping requires an informed consumer. How does one get more information? By consulting a physician, a dietitian, an exercise physiologist, or a certified athletic trainer. Credible sources may also be found on the internet. An intelligent research reader looks at who funded the research, the number of subjects, whether or not there was a control group, and the research conclusions. Just reading the abstract of the research isn't enough; the entire document should be critically examined.

Some sports supplements are marketed as "prohormones." These are essentially a naturally occurring form of anabolic steroid. Once ingested, prohomones convert by normal metabolic processes into active anabolic compounds, also called target hormones. The process requires enzymes found naturally within the body. Prohormones need these enzymes, but the enzymes are limited in the amount of hormone they can convert in a given time.

This conversion process that takes place in the body is what distinguishes prohormones from true anabolic steroids and allows prohormones to remain "legal"—though this is under increasing legislative scrutiny. The downside of the conversion process is that the required enzymes become saturated at a certain point, necessarily limiting the amount of active hormone that can effectively be used in any given period of time. Because of this dose ceiling, there is a limit on how much one can increase prohormone doses for enhanced results.

Once converted into active hormones, prohormones interact with what are called androgen receptors, just as anabolic steroids do. The stimulation of androgen receptors, located throughout the body, triggers the anabolic effect that is responsible for the size and strength gains associated with anabolic steroids.

User of prohormones should abide by the same medical safety precautions—liver function tests and blood monitoring—as described earlier for users of anabolic steroids. Prohormones stretch the dietary supplement law to the limit without totally breaking it, because they do contain amino acids and minerals.

Here are the categories within which most sports supplements fall:

Muscle Growth and Weight Gain: These products contain primarily amino acids. They often contain significantly high amounts of sugars in the form of fructose, dextrose, or sucrose. Remember that anything the body does not use for energy or eliminate is stored as fat.

Weight Loss: Two years ago, many of these supplements contained ephedra. But after the death of baseball player Steve Bechler, ephedra was removed from them, though it is still readily available elsewhere. Now these products usually contain chromium picolinate, creatine monohydrate, caffeine, and green tea extract. The term "thermogenic" (fat burning) popularly describes these substances.

Chromium supplements come in several forms, never as pure chromium. You can buy chromium picolinate, chromium chloride, chromium nicotinate, and high-chromium yeast. Nicotinate and picolinate seem more easily absorbed than the others. There are some safety concerns about chromium picolinate, since laboratory studies have found that it may damage genetic material in animal cells, which suggests it could cause cancer or fertility problems in offspring. It seems to be the combination of chromium and picolinate that's the potential problem, not the chromium alone. Of course, what happens in a test tube or in lab animals may not happen in the human body; but there is potential for risk with chromium picolinate, particularly in large doses or over the long term.

Hemodilators: In this relatively new category, the products are expensive. These substances purport to open or widen blood vessels, thus increasing blood flow and producing an enhanced "pumped" appearance long after a workout. Hemodilators are the current "hot item" in sports supplements, with wild claims being made for their effects. Supplements tend to follow almost faddish patterns of creation, hysteria, and reduction, so it may be premature to jump on the bandwagon. The primary ingredients in these products are amino acids.

Energy Enhancers: These products usually contain caffeine. They can range from simple pills or "Red Bull"–type energy drinks to near-toxic levels of combined substances intended to enhance concentration and wakefulness.

Creatine Products: These products contain creatine either in monohydrate, dicreatine citrate, or buffered monohydrate forms. They are marketed for muscle growth and performance enhancement. Research studies have indicated that athletes taking creatine products should drink water regularly to avoid muscle cramps.

Dehydroepiandrosterone (DHEA): This natural steroid hormone is produced from cholesterol by the adrenal glands. DHEA is chemically similar to testosterone and estrogen and is easily converted into those hormones. DHEA production peaks in early adulthood and declines with age in both men and women. Thus many diseases associated with aging also correlate with low levels of DHEA production. Advocates of DHEA recommend it to prevent the effects of aging. There has been no scientific evidence, however, that low levels of DHEA are a significant factor in the development of diseases associated with aging. Nor is there any evidence that increasing DHEA slows down, stops, or reverses the aging process. Unfortunately there is no fountain of youth in a bottle. DHEA has been specifically excluded from several recent legislative initiatives due to extensive lobbying.

Human Growth Hormone (HGH): This is the most abundant hormone produced by the pituitary gland, located in the center of the brain. HGH is also a very complex hormone. It consists of 191 amino acids, making it fairly large for a hormone. In fact it is the largest protein created by the pituitary gland. HGH secretion reaches its peak in the body during adolescence. This makes sense because HGH helps stimulate body growth. But HGH secretion continues after adolescence, usually in short bursts during deep sleep. Growth hormone is known to be critical for tissue repair, muscle growth, healing, brain function, physical and mental health, bone strength, energy, and metabolism.

You will not find true human growth hormone in a bottle in tablet form, despite labeling. If it were true HGH, it would be a full-blown hormone and not a dietary supplement, and therefore available only by prescription, usually in a liquid form. If a company claims to have a significant amount of HGH in its products, it is less than truthful. HGH is a prescription drug. If you were to put significant amounts of HGH into a dietary supplement, it would no longer be a supplement but a drug. As a drug it must meet FDA approval and may be sold only by prescription. So, essentially, the phrase "HGH dietary supplement" is an oxymoron.

Most supplements will attempt artfully to suggest that HGH is an ingredient without saying so explicitly. Those who wish to use HGH will usually turn to the black market rather than use readily available supplements.

Because HGH is a delicate and complex 191 amino acid hormone, it cannot be taken orally. Even if a company wanted to break the law and sell HGH as a pill, spray, or powder, it would not work because the HGH would break down before it ever reached the bloodstream, nullifying its beneficial effect. Finally, pure HGH in a recombinant or synthesized form is extremely expensive. Some clinics charge their patients more than $2,000 a month for injections of HGH. Obviously that kind of pricing does not work well in the over-the-counter supplement market.

Under current federal law, any dietary supplement may be marketed without advance testing, unlike prescription medications that must undergo a three-stage testing process before being brought to market. The only current restriction on supplements is that the label may not claim the product will treat, prevent, or cure a disease. But the label may use vague claims like "enhances energy" or "supports testosterone production." If serious problems are reported, it's up to the Food and Drug Administration to prove they are real before it can order a supplement off the market or impose other restrictions. So far, that has happened infrequently. Only the recent removal of ephedra-based products by the FDA stands as testament that it is even possible.

But a few manufacturers have voluntarily recalled their supplements after the FDA warned them of possible dangers. In March 2004 the FDA concluded that there is inadequate information to confirm that a dietary supplement containing androstenedione can reasonably be expected to be safe. In fact, the FDA believes that these products may increase the risk of serious health problems because they are converted in the body to testosterone, which is an androgenic and anabolic steroid.

Another way to examine sport supplements is to look at the claims made for the products, then compare them to the scientific findings regarding those claims. The following chart illustrates this:

SUPPLEMENT	CLAIM	SCIENTIFIC EVIDENCE
Protein powders	Builds muscles through protein synthesis	Excess may convert to fat, cause dehydration, and lead to cramping
Caffeine	Improves endurance and alertness, aids weight loss	USOC banned if amount equals 8 cups coffee; may cause diuretic effects, muscle tremors
L-Carnitine	Promotes lean body mass	Body produces sufficient amount; any extra does not cause increased thermogenic effect
Chromium	Builds muscles, aids weight loss	Co-factor for insulin action; dietary deficiencies rare; evidence does not support claims; picolinate form may be unsafe
Creatine	Improves anaerobic performance, builds muscles	Can improve performance for short bursts; possible dehydration side effects, including muscle cramping; rehydration very important when using creatine
Ginseng	Improves energy	No proven studies— possibility of dehyration effect

Now we look at some of the specific sports supplements available. These have been chosen because they are widely distributed and represent the classifications just described. We make no representation, either expressed or implied, regarding the nutritional value of these supplements, or whether or not anyone should purchase them. The products are identified by brand name, manufacturer, amount in bottle/can, approximate price (prices tend to vary depending on point of purchase), dosage, advertising claims, ingredients, and cost for a year's indicated dosage.

Product name: Creatine Plus
- *Manufacturer*: EAS
- *Amount*: 30 ounces
- *Approximate cost*: $15
- *Dosage*: 172 grams per day (6 ounces)
- *Advertising claim*: "Boosts muscle size and strength"
- *Ingredients*: Dextrose, a sugar
  □ Chromium monohydrate, mineral
  □ Taurine, sulfur amino acid
- *Cost per year*: $1,095

Product name: Carb Dynam X
- *Manufacturer*: EAS
- *Amount*: 60 capsules
- *Approximate cost*: $11
- *Dosage*: 9 capsules per day
- *Advertising claim*: "Body shaper, minimizes body fat storage"
- *Ingredients*: Chromium amino acid chelate, 200 mcg (amino acid chelate is the product resulting from the reaction of a metal ion from a soluble metal salt with amino acids)
  □ Umbrella Arum Root, 1,200 mg, tropical botanical

- ☐ Cinnamon bark, 400 mg, herb to aid digestion
- ☐ Fenugreek seed, 300 mg, herb to soothe the stomach
- *Cost per year*: $605

Product name: Ripped Fuel
- *Manufacturer*: Twinlab
- *Amount*: 60 capsules
- *Approximate cost*: $14
- *Dosage*: 6 capsules per day
- *Advertising claim*: "Fat metabolizer and metabolic enhancer"
- *Ingredients*: Guarana seed extract, 800 mg, herbal stimulant
  - ☐ Bitter orange fruit extract, 325 mg, herb used in traditional Chinese medicine
  - ☐ L-phenylanine, 50 mg, essential amino acid
- *Cost per year*: $504

Product name: NOS
- *Manufacturer*: Healthwatchers
- *Amount*: 180 tablets
- *Approximate cost*: $28
- *Dosage*: 9 tablets per day
- *Advertising claim*: "Supports nitric oxide synthesis"
- *Ingredients*: L-arginine alpha ketoglutarate, 3 grams, nonessential amino acid
- *Cost per year*: $532

Product name: CLA (Conjugated Linoleic Acid)
- *Manufacturer*: EAS
- *Amount*: 60 softgels
- *Approximate cost*: $15
- *Dosage*: 4 softgels per day
- *Advertising claim*: "Fat burner"

- *Ingredients*: Conjugated Linoleic Acid, fatty acid found in red meat and cheese
- *Cost per year*: $360

Product name: Hydroxycut
- *Manufacturer*: Muscletech
- *Amount*: 58 capsules
- *Approximate cost*: $25
- *Dosage*: 9 capsules per day
- *Advertising claim*: "Weight loss"
- *Ingredients*: Green tea extract, botanical tea leaf extract
- *Cost per year*: $1,525

Product name: Universal Animal Stak 2
- *Manufacturer*: Universal Nutrition
- *Amount*: 44 packs
- *Approximate cost*: $60
- *Dosage*: 1 pack per day
- *Advertising claim*: "Accelerated amino acid transport"
- *Ingredients*: Chromium picolinate, 1,000 mcg, mineral
  - Magnesium oxide, 450 mg, mineral
  - Longjack extract complex, 250 mg, herb
- *Cost per year*: $240

Product name: Tribulus Terrestris
- *Manufacturer*: Sci-Fit
- *Amount*: 60 capsules
- *Approximate cost*: $20
- *Dosage*: 2 capsules per day
- *Advertising claim*: "Testosterone enhancer"
- *Ingredients*: Tribulis terrestris, 500 mg, herb
- *Cost per year*: $240

Product name: Vast 2
- *Manufacturer*: Prolab

- *Amount*: 180 capsules
- *Approximate cost*: $27
- *Dosage*: 6 capsules per day
- *Advertising claim*: "Serious muscle hardness"
- *Ingredients*: Taurine, 800 mg, amino acid
  - Silenium, 33 mcg, mineral
  - Venadyl sulfate, 7.5 mg, mineral
- *Cost per year*: $324

Product name: HMB
- *Manufacturer*: EAS
- *Amount*: 200 capsules
- *Approximate cost*: $40
- *Dosage*: 12 capsules per day
- *Advertising claim*: "Active repair, protein breakdown suppressor"
- *Ingredients*: B-hydroxy B-methylbutyrate monohydrate, 1 gram, amino acid
  - Potassium phosphate, 200 mg, electrolyte
  - Calcium from tri-calcium phosphate, 200 mg
- *Cost per year*: $667

Product name: Synthevol 2
- *Manufacturer*: EAS
- *Amount*: 32 ounces
- *Approximate price*: $60
- *Dosage*: 90 grams per day (approx. 3 ounces)
- *Advertising claim*: "Increases lean body mass and enhances performance"
- *Ingredients*: Creatine Monohydrate, 10 grams, creatine
  - Sugars, 10 grams, carbohydrate
  - Glutanine, 6 grams, amino acid
  - Taurine, 2 grams, amino acid
- *Cost per year*: $2,160

Product name: Mega Creatine
- *Manufacturer*: GNC
- *Amount*: 20 1-ounce packets
- *Approximate cost*: $28
- *Dosage*: 1 packet per day
- *Advertising claim*: "Energy production during exercise, may improve athletic performance"
- *Ingredients*: Dextrose, 12 grams, a sugar
  - DiCreatine citrate, 5 grams, creatine
  - Potassium, 600 mg, electrolyte
- *Cost per year*: $511

Product name: MS Extreme
- *Manufacturer*: Cellucor
- *Amount*: 180 grams (approx. 6 fluid ounces)
- *Approximate cost*: $60
- *Dosage*: 2 tablespoons (1 ounce) per day with water
- *Advertising claim*: "Increased energy"
- *Ingredients*: Proprietary blend of:
  - Buffered creatine monohydrate, creatine
  - Glycocyamine, amino acid
  - Silica hydroxide, mineral
- *Cost per year*: $3,650

Product name: L Glutamine 1500
- *Manufacturer*: Now Sports
- *Amount*: 90 tablets
- *Approximate cost*: $30
- *Dosage*: 4 tablets per day
- *Advertising claim*: "Supports muscle mass"
- *Ingredients*: L-glutamine, 3 grams, amino acid
  - Stearic acid, saturated fatty acid
- *Cost per year*: $498

Product name: Amino Burst 3000
- *Manufacturer*: GNC
- *Amount*: 90 tablets
- *Dosage*: 3 tablets per day
- *Approximate cost*: $17
- *Advertising claim*: "Muscle builder"
- *Ingredients*: L-carnitine, 15 mg, amino acid
  □ Whey protein, 3 grams, protein source
  □ Glutamic acid, 190 mg, amino acid
- *Cost per year*: $207

Product name: NO2 Hemodilator
- *Manufacturer*: MRI
- *Amount*: 180 caplets
- *Dosage*: 10 caplets per day
- *Approximate cost*: $80
- *Advertising claim*: "Amplifies growth signal, accelerates fast-twitch strength, aids recovery"
- *Ingredients*: Arginine as Alphaketoglutarate, amino acid
  □ Calcium phosphate, mineral salt
  □ Seaweed extract, organic nutrient
- *Cost per year*: $1,622

Again, these products are merely representative of what is available on the sports supplement market. Before deciding on the need for a supplement and which one is most appropriate, people should chart their food intake and exercise routine, including a calculation of the number of calories consumed and burned off. (Books and information available on the internet, as well as doctors and registered dietitians, can help.) Then they should look at the nutrition pyramid for active people and see if their diet is deficient in any area. If so, they have two choices: (1) change the diet, or (2) supplement to make up the deficiencies.

Next, look at exercise goals. Unless individuals plan to do heavy resistance more than three times per week, their diet should be sufficient to support a workout program. If goals include gaining muscle mass, they may need to supplement with an amino acid product to minimize muscle breakdown from the heavy resistance program they will use.

Whatever the exercise goals, an aerobic aspect (cardiovascular fitness) will most likely be needed at least thirty minutes a day, five times a week, plus a flexibility program. A physician should be consulted before starting or changing any exercise plan.

Supplements are not magic potions; they can't take a person beyond the limits of his or her genetic code. But they can support a well-planned exercise program and benefit a physically active individual when used properly and intelligently.

Homework and research should precede the purchase of supplements. Product claims should be scrutinized, clerks should be asked about details. Ingredients may be copied down and checked in a supplement guide or on the internet (but not on manufacturer/seller sites) before purchase. Others should be asked about their experience with the product. These tactics will make for informed consumers who will be able to make intelligent decisions about supplements.

Many people forget to check the expiration date when they purchase a supplement. They may pay good money for expired ingredients. And consumers should be careful about buying on the internet. If a price looks too good to be true, it probably is. Supplement counterfeiters operate on the internet, selling outdated products or supplements that do not contain what they advertise.

Supplements can add to a healthy diet and exercise program, but all too often they are viewed as a shortcut, like other performance-enhancing drugs. It's part of our chemical culture to look for a pill rather than put in time and effort. Add greed to this mix and there's potential for abuse. Supplement manufacturers churn out new products with every new fad or desire. It says something that after ephedra was banned by the government in 2004, there was a run on supplement stores to "stock up" before the ban took effect. Even before the ban, products such as Xenadrine had replaced their active ingredient and become "ephedra free—even more effective!"

Used properly, there is a place for supplements. Used improperly, they are at best a waste, at worst a gateway to stronger, more dangerous drugs. This industry is ripe for regulation.

7

Profile: The Tester

"WE'RE ALWAYS a little bit behind." That phrase kept recurring as I spoke with people in the drug-testing profession. The continual game of cat and mouse that drug testers play with drug users makes me wonder which one is the cat. Given the rules the drug testers currently play under, you might wonder too.

Drug testing is a difficult occupation, much like being a detective. Testers are supposed to collect evidence, conduct research, and present findings in order to catch rule breakers. Worse, most of them are asked to do all this and turn a profit.

As some users of performance-enhancing drugs sign multi-million-dollar contracts and endorsement deals, basking in the glow of adulation and applause, the testers are there too, waiting in the wings to collect their samples. It's a small field with few credible operators; the fingers of one hand are all you need to count them.

I had an opportunity to speak with Dr. David L. Black, president of Aegis Sciences Corporation, one of the few companies with the experience and federal certification that allows them to test elite-level athletes as well as working with corporate and academic clients. Located in Nashville, Tennessee, the company offers what it calls "Zero-Tolerance Drug Testing," a program that is touted as the most accurate drug-testing program available. (Black does not conduct testing for Major League Baseball. A lab in Montreal handles that.)

"We handle work only when the results of our efforts may be involved in a legal proceeding that could be criminal or civil, or an administrative hearing," Black told me. "So we provide not only laboratory services that will generate information to be used in an accusation of drug use. We also serve as an expert witness on occasion when someone needs the services of a company with our background to help explain or defend a case."

Black is regarded as one of the leading drug-testing officials in the world. In my research, his name came up again and again among people involved in this issue, from all sides. "How did you get involved in drug testing?" I asked.

"Well, my doctorate is from the University of Maryland School of Medicine, in forensic toxicology. I'm a board-certified forensic toxicologist as well as a board-certified clinical toxicologist. I have a fair amount of experience in the whole issue of doping control and the use of drugs in sports as well as experience in post-mortem death investigation and workplace drug testing, high school programs, policy development and testing, and working with law enforcement, at both federal and state levels." Black clearly has credentials and experience.

I asked him if there were other companies similar to Aegis. "It depends on which application you're interested in," he said. "With regard to testing for drugs in the workplace there are forty-nine U.S. laboratories certified by the federal government. In the arena of drug-free sports there are only four legitimate players in North America that can provide the service where an appropriate investment has been made."

I asked, "Do you believe that drugs in sports—such as steroids and other performance enhancers—are a significant problem?"

"Yes! The problem goes beyond steroids and other performance-enhancing drugs," he replied. "Of course there are drugs used in training that generate thoughts of anabolic steroids. But the much larger problem is drug use at the time of competition. So yes, it's a significant problem."

Black was willing to discuss various types of drugs that were in use, distinguishing among them rather than shoving them under one metaphorical umbrella. I asked him what drugs he saw as the biggest problems. It didn't surprise me that steroids were not the first ones he mentioned. Instead he said immediately: stimulants.

"Stimulants have been a problem of long standing—amphetamines and other substances. Caffeine has been used historically to enhance performance. More recently the World Anti-Doping Association has taken caffeine off the banned list. But caffeine remains a stimulant and can certainly affect performance when used at certain levels. Narcotics that allow an athlete to play through the pain are also an important issue.

"More recently we are seeing the introduction of more complicated medications, like synthetic EPO as a blood-doping agent. It can increase the oxygen-carrying capacity of the blood compartment, so it's used in endurance sports. Human growth hormone has been a problem for a long time—and very, very difficult to test for. Other drugs—beta blockers and diuretics—are used too, especially in weight-classification events like boxing or wrestling. When you look at the various sports, then add up the number of drugs that can be found in them, you come up with several thousand medications that can be used to attempt to enhance performance."

That's a daunting number. It's precisely this problem of scale that puts the tester at a disadvantage. "How much of a problem is it that you have so many substances to test for?"

"It surely is a challenge," he said, with a faint sigh. What he was about to tell me was surprising. "But it's not often that we actually test for all those drugs."

I kept my mouth from dropping open. "What?"

"Usually there is a very defined, focused intent from whichever sports organization we're working with. Usually the focus is on anabolic steroids, then on drugs that are not necessarily used for performance enhancement—social drugs like marijuana or cocaine," Black continued. "Currently only major amateur athletic competitive events like the Olympic Games search for a wide range of drugs. And yes, we lag behind those who choose to cheat because the testing programs target specific drugs.

"We do not routinely test in a nontargeted fashion. Nontargeted testing is a far more expensive process. It could be done, and it might help shorten the time between the introduction of a new drug and our ability to identify its use. But the cost consideration is significant. Cost usually drives the decision to test for particular drugs. So yes, those who choose to cheat know what we are targeting, what drugs we are trying to identify. They look for drugs within the same drug class that are not currently being targeted."

I wanted to know more about how testing is done. If all drugs aren't being tested for, how does this work? "When you get a sample from a sports organization, roughly how many different tests are you running on that sample?"

Again, there was no simple answer. "It depends on how we define a test. For instance, with anabolic steroids we do a test that would be defined as a "profile," and we call it a profile because there are forty-three or forty-four different elements to that profile. There's a testing not only for the testosterone and the epitestosterone, looking at the ratio between the two, but then also the synthetic steroids like stanazolol—which is also known as Winstrol—Deca-Durabolin, and a few others. When we look for the synthetic drugs, the organization will usually give us one, two, or three metabolites to look for.

"So we are actually looking for a good number of elements in a profile. Now also, depending upon the client, we may be assessing a sample for water content. If a sample is diluted, the client may want a test for diuretics, which might be used to increase the water content of a urine sample. By increasing the water content you bring down the concentration of the drug, and that could cause us to miss the presence of, say, a targeted steroid. Within the steroid profile we also look for a blocking drug that might be used by an athlete to try to block the release of the drug out of the body through the urine."

I wanted a clarification. "These blocking drugs—are they what we normally refer to as a masking agent?"

"Correct," he answered. "We also look for evidence of the introduction of chemicals into the urine sample at time of collection. The subject of the test may be using oxidizers, trying to destroy the drugs we're looking for. Then we also go though specimen validity tests. We have to test to verify that we really did receive a correct urine sample, because people do try to substitute someone else's sample at time of collection." In fact, the sale of urine is a profitable sideline for some day-care facilities: five-year-olds tend to have clean urine.

"What's the procedure you go through to make sure you have a valid sample?"

"In the sports testing arena most of the samples we are provided have been collected under either direct observation or certainly with a closely escorted process in the collection site. . . ."

I interrupted him: "Direct observation is just that—they're watching the sample come out?"

"Exactly. They are watching the void of the sample from the body into the cup. The athlete is involved in the process at the moment of collection. The athlete participates in that process by signing paperwork documenting that he or she has witnessed the process of collection, that the sample being identified is in fact that individual's sample. On the multi-part form used in the collection process, the athlete signs a statement that he has seen nothing occur in the collection process that would make him believe the sample is not his. The completion of the paperwork is witnessed, and the paperwork then accompanies the sample to the laboratory.

"At the collection site the sample is sealed with a security seal and placed in a container, then that's placed in a shipping container which is also sealed. The sample must be received at the laboratory with the seals intact and with the appropriate paperwork for the sample that was collected." That sounded to me more like a law-enforcement chain of custody than something I'd expect, but in fact it's much the same because the eventual judgment could very well end up in a court of law.

Now that it was collected, I wondered how fast a sample could be tested and returned. How long did it take to turn around the test?

"There's not necessarily an easy answer," Black told me. "On anabolic steroids, a negative testing would take approximately three days to get a report back to the institution. A positive testing would take perhaps another three to four days to generate the report. We have to check and double-check positives. They are screened by gas chromatography and mass spectrometry, and then there's a confirming test once there's a positive finding on the screening test. There has to be a repeat analysis on the gas chromatography and mass spectrometry equipment. That's a pretty labor-intensive process in terms of sample preparation as well as documentation.

"With regard to other drugs, it depends again on which drugs we are focusing on. If it's the social drugs like marijuana and cocaine and amphetamines, methamphetamines, ecstasy, eve, adam—those drugs can be screened in one day and a negative answer provided the next day. If it's positive on the screening test, a confirmation can be accomplished within twenty-four to forty-eight hours. It's a much faster turnaround time principally because some of the drugs we would be looking for have simpler screening systems available. The screening systems for anabolic steroids or even something like diuretics or beta blockers are quite complex. Some of these drug classes require a very sophisticated analytical approach in order to turn the test result around."

Many of the steroid users and anti-testing advocates I'd spoken to had said they opposed testing for two main reasons: invasion of privacy and the frequency of false positives. I asked Dr. Black how much of a problem these false positives were.

He had a ready answer. "Because of the science that's used in testing today, and the kind of work we're doing, the probability of a false positive finding from the science side of the equation is pretty minimal because of the molecular fingerprint. The ultimate identification is done by a very specific, very sensitive, and very sophisticated technology—gas chromatography and mass spectrometry. When we look at that data, we know it's associated with the chemical we have now identified. Whether it's an anabolic steroid, marijuana, or a cocaine by-product in the body, we have a molecular fingerprint that is unique. That won't be misidentified."

Still, there could be a problem. "There are two better opportunities for a so-called false positive. One would be at the collection site. The process we go through—the one I've described to you in detail—really minimizes that opportunity. The other possibility would be misinterpreting the data. Our greatest difficulty is with supplements and nutritional products from the marketplace that contain legitimate substances which inside the body break down into banned substances. We have seen a number of professional and amateur athletes accused of using drugs to enhance performance when in fact what they did is take a poorly researched, poorly labeled, or poorly manufactured supplement."

"In my research, mass spectrometry appeared to be the most sophisticated testing technique in use," Black explained. "Mass spectrometry has been applied for a number of years. It's the gold standard not only for drug testing but also for research purposes in other applications. Much depends on the type of equipment. Some instruments can be purchased for as little as $80,000." That doesn't sound so little to me, and it may explain why there are so few drug-testing labs.

"But there are other instrument systems. Depending on what drugs you're looking for and what your detection limits are, instruments may need to be applied that could cost as much as, say, $300,000 or $400,000. So it depends upon the drug being targeted and the degree of sensitivity requested. Even in this gold-standard technology, there is continual improvement in instruments. It's a very sophisticated technology and elegant in the information it generates."

Unfortunately the drug problem has descended from the elite and professional levels, through the colleges and into the high schools, and even lower. With the new public awareness of the problem, I had seen some home tests that are being marketed even to Little League parents. Given the complexity and cost of the equipment Dr. Black had spoken of, I asked if these types of tests had any legitimate accuracy?

"It's disappointing that the Food and Drug Administration has allowed these products into the marketplace, because they generate both false positives and false negatives," Black explained. "They can falsely alarm a parent if food or other products that a child may be using create a false positive. They can also give false comfort to a parent by providing a false negative. When we use instruments in a laboratory that cost from $80,000 to $400,000, I'm sure you can well imagine how hard it is put that kind of accuracy and precise analysis into a $5 or $10 throwaway device. It's just— it's not there. This is quite different from a pregnancy test!"

The issue of cost was also true of the professional tests. I asked, "When an agency comes to you and says we want to do a drug test on an athlete, what kind of cost is it looking at?"

"I'm not the one who ordinarily quotes prices!" Black confessed. "We do have a profile for anabolic steroids that is more restricted. It was developed for high school applications so that those programs could find it affordable. It targets the substances that have been identified in the United States as being commonly used—as opposed to looking for all the steroids used internationally. I believe that particular test is somewhere around $85 to $90 per sample. That's a considerable reduction from the standard fee for an androgenic-anabolic steroid test of about $195 list."

Cost would obviously be a major issue for a high school, where budgets are often the deciding factor in far too many decisions. For a professional sports application, $200 doesn't seem like much. Major League Baseball has about 1,500 players they would need to test. A million dollars would test each of those players three times and still leave money for research and education.

Black agreed. "For professional sports, frankly, I guess it all depends on perspective. It's always simple to spend other people's money, but the amount of money spent elsewhere will always dwarf what goes into even a very aggressive testing program. In the economic trickle-down of this whole business, the laboratory is the last trickle in the process. It's just hard to imagine it could be a point of debate. The amount of money involved in sports is simply incredible. For football, it's never been an issue. For baseball . . ." His voice trailed off.

Black also had some thoughts about the recent furor over designer steroids, especially the best known, THG. I asked him, "How long does it take to develop a new test once you have a sample of the drug to work from?"

"That's not necessarily an easy task," he said. "The World Anti-Doping Association benefited tremendously by having an individual who came into possession of a syringe with THG in it, and he gave it to a laboratory for testing. That's a huge advantage because it gives you an enormous concentration of the drug. To identify properly, and do all the science associated with identifying an unknown compound, you have to figure several weeks at least, perhaps more.

"It depends on your resources, and how much computer power you can bring to the investigation, and the level of expertise of the scientists engaged in the inquiry. It could take several weeks simply to identify what the pure substance is. Then you have to develop a method for looking at how that drug would travel through the body. We'd have to answer what the potential metabolites or by-products out of the body might be. We'd have to design a process that we would use with a urine sample to isolate the drug. We'd have to purify that sample before we could introduce the extract onto an instrument like a gas chromatograph or mass spectrometer.

"It might take weeks or even months to develop that process. Then you have to validate it. You have to be sure that other drugs cannot interfere. You have to demonstrate certain characteristics of the test, like lower limits of detection, upper limits of quantification, and the precision of analysis both within the run and between runs. It gets rather sophisticated and complicated just to validate the method, so you are talking about several months of effort."

If the track coach Trevor Graham hadn't sent along the vial of THG, would it have been detected? "Probably not. No."

Black had earlier touched on the issue of detecting human growth hormone. The IOC and WADA had announced, just before the 2004 Olympics in Athens, that they would be testing for HGH. While it had already been a banned substance, there had been no valid test. What raised eyebrows was that at the time of the announcement, there *still* was no valid test. Black explained the current state of HGH testing. "First, everyone needs to understand that it's going to be a blood test, not a urine test. Baseball, I understand, bans HGH but doesn't have a protocol for blood testing. That's toothless, but understandable. Until there's a valid test, there's really nothing more than a statement to be made anyway. Right now, existing tests simply measure against a baseline, and they're poor quality. The tests are not forensically acceptable at this stage. It will take a lot more research. About the only positive step the Olympics took was to save some samples for later testing.

"I'm not sure if they intend to take away medals at a later stage, but testing is about two things: identification and intimidation. We identify those we can, and we hope that the threat of testing and penalties will prevent others from using. That's the ideal."

As my conversation with Dr. Black drew to a close, it seemed like the cat-and-mouse game was not so much a game but an inevitability. I asked him if he felt drug testers are doomed forever to pursue drug users. He smiled. "Probably, but that's not so bad. We need more funds. We need to develop new tests, new procedures, speed up the processes, train more people. We need to get serious about education and research, to be pro-active rather than forever reactive. We need to worry about new techniques like genetic doping. Ten years ago we had blood doping, now we have EPO. Five years ago we had Deca and Winstrol, now we have THG. Two years ago we had amphetamines, now we have Modanifil. The target is always moving, and science has to move with it, aiming just ahead. Our society will never be drug-free and probably never really accept a zero tolerance. Sport is entertainment, after all, and drug testing injects a bit too much reality for most of them. We can't rid ourselves of tobacco and alcohol, two well-documented public and personal health risks. Can we expect more of sport?"

8

A Comparison:
Football's Steroids Policy

IN 1985 the biggest celebrity on the Chicago Bears was the rookie defensive tackle William "The Refrigerator" Perry. Fans loved Perry not because he was the best player on the great Bears' defense (far from it) or because he was occasionally called on to carry the ball at the goal line. Fans loved Perry because he was huge. No one could get over how enormous the Fridge was. The very idea of a man that huge inspired laughter and even awe among the fans.

Perry weighed an even three hundred pounds.

Five years later, in 1990, the National Football League had thirty-five players who weighed three hundred pounds or more. At the start of the 2005 season, there are so many three-hundred-pounders that among linemen it would be easier to count those who weigh *less* than three hundred pounds; the league has at least three hundred players who top the three-hundred-pound mark.

The number of players in the NFL who weigh three hundred pounds has exploded in the same way that the fifty-home-run season in baseball has become more common. Yet we don't hear anything close to the number of allegations of pharmaceutical enhancement in football that we hear in baseball. Is that because the players in football aren't juiced, or because the NFL is better at public relations than Major League Baseball?

No one can dispute that football's policy against steroids is much tougher than baseball's. The NFL, which started testing for steroids in 1987, had a fifteen-year head start on Major League Baseball. The NFL separates its tests for steroids and other performance-enhancing drugs from its tests for cocaine, marijuana, and other recreational drugs, and it treats players who test positive for steroids much more harshly than it treats players who test positive for recreational drugs.

For recreational drugs, the league informs players in advance when they will be tested. Players who test positive once are directed to counseling; no one is suspended from the league until he has tested positive at least twice.

With drugs classified as performance-enhancing, which includes steroids but also stimulants including ephedrine, the NFL is much stricter. Every week the league tests six randomly selected players from each team; most players get tested twice a season with no advance notice. A player who tests positive is suspended for four games the first time, six games the second time, and indefinitely—but at least one year—the third time. A four-game suspension in the NFL, with its sixteen-game seasons, also means forfeiting one-fourth of the player's annual salary. An equivalent suspension for baseball would be forty games for the first offense.

Some players and observers have criticized the league for separating performance-enhancing drugs from recreational drugs. The Carolina Panthers defensive end Julius Peppers was suspended for the last four games of his rookie season when he tested positive for a legal, over-the-counter dietary supplement that included a stimulant on the NFL's banned list. Peppers bristled that his punishment for taking something that he viewed as no different from a vitamin supplement was to miss a quarter of the season, whereas if he had smoked crack or used heroin he would have gotten off with a warning. The real difference in the NFL lies not in the policy but in the relationship between the league and the players' union. Any player who went to his union to try to reduce the league's penalties for using performance-enhancing drugs wouldn't just have to fight the owners, he'd also have to go through many of his fellow players. In the NFL some of the most vocal proponents of steroid testing were players who supported it because they feared being injured by juiced-up opponents. A football player who has to line up against someone who is using steroids is at an increased risk of getting hurt. A baseball player doesn't have to worry about intentional collisions with someone who's bigger, stronger, and faster because of steroids.

Gene Upshaw, a Hall of Fame offensive lineman and the head of the players' union, resisted steroid testing when Pete Rozelle, NFL commissioner at the time, first suggested it. But Upshaw and his union considered the injury concerns of players and quickly decided not to fight the league on the issue. If the league's drug tests are to be believed, the NFL's performance-enhancing drug policy is working. According to published reports, the league on average has fewer than five positive tests a year. This doesn't match up with the increasing size of the players.

One reason football has been far ahead of Major League Baseball in its steroid testing is the presence of cautionary tales throughout the league:

  * Steve Courson, a 275-pound lineman who was best known for his play with the Pittsburgh Steelers in the 1970s, became one of the first people to address the use of steroids in pro football when he admitted at the end of his career in 1985 that he had used steroids. He said he had started using them in college at South

Carolina and used them throughout his NFL career. He also said he thought at least half of his fellow NFL players used steroids— a chilling parallel to Ken Caminiti's claims about Major League Baseball. After retiring, Courson experienced serious heart problems that he linked to his use of steroids. Once on a heart transplant list, Courson has now regained his health through diet and exercise. He speaks to young people about the dangers of steroids, but he also points out that their major risk is that they are used in extremely high, unmonitored dosages.

* Former Cardinals lineman Bob Young entered the NFL in 1964 as a nineteenth-round draft choice and had a fairly quiet career for more than a decade, but in his thirties he became significantly stronger and was a first-time All-Pro at age thirty-seven. Young died at fifty-two, and his family blamed his steroid use, though he also had diabetes and was a heavy smoker.

* In 1988 *Sports Illustrated* featured the first-person account of former South Carolina defensive lineman Tommy Chaikin's experience with steroids, which he said led him to illness, violence, and a suicide attempt. That article led to a scandal that cost everyone on the South Carolina coaching staff his job. Three coaches pleaded guilty to steroid charges.

* Former Denver Broncos, Cleveland Browns, and Los Angeles Raiders defensive lineman Lyle Alzado died at age forty-three in 1992 of brain cancer that he attributed to his steroid use. *Sports Illustrated* featured Alzado on its cover with the words, "I lied." Alzado became the poster boy for the hazards of steroids, though some doctors questioned whether steroid use caused his cancer. Alzado is also an example of why steroid users can't be identified simply by their size. He weighed 254 pounds—too small to be a defensive lineman today.

* Hall of Fame center Mike Webster of the 1970s Pittsburgh Steelers said steroids were in part to blame for the severe mental

and physical health problems he suffered after retiring. Webster, who played alongside Courson for several years, died in 2002.

Aside from body weight, football also lacks a statistical measuring stick that fans can use to gauge the strength of the players. Baseball has a statistic that easily measures whether players are getting stronger: home runs.

When you're told that before 1998 no one could hit more than sixty-one home runs in a season, and that from 1998 to 2001 it happened six times, you feel confident saying the players are getting stronger and questioning how that has happened. It may not be provable or even true, but that's the perception. In football the players most likely to use steroids are offensive and defensive linemen. If those players get stronger via steroids, their gains in strength will merely cancel each other out, and there will be no noticeable difference in the statistics.

One of the few nonlinemen who has been busted for steroids is wide receiver David Boston. Playing with the Arizona Cardinals, Boston looked like one of the league's young rising stars in 2001, his third NFL season, when he led the league with 1,598 receiving yards. His bubble burst a bit in 2002 when he missed eight games due to injury and clashed with his coaches, making his exit as a free agent no cause for Cardinals tears. After signing with San Diego, Boston's weight traveled north of 260 pounds; he looked more like a competitive bodybuilder than a football player. His enormous muscles didn't help him much as he suffered through a string of injuries in one forgettable season with the Chargers. Boston, now with the Miami Dolphins, missed all of the 2004 season with a knee injury. In February 2005 he pleaded no contest to a charge that he struck a ticket agent at the Burlington (Vermont) International Airport, where he was traveling for rehabilitation on his knee. Boston's injuries and anger-management problem seem to point to the classic side effects of his proven steroid use.

Do suspensions like Boston's show that the NFL's policy works to prevent steroid users from playing in the league? Or do we cynically say that the NFL wants its drug policy to make its fans believe the players aren't using steroids, rather than actually to stop players from using steroids? Courson has said he thinks the NFL is more interested in public relations than in effective drug policy. Sports leagues sell entertainment, and if fans perceive the game on the field as tainted, the leagues are in trouble.

For the past few decades the NFL has been much better at public relations than Major League Baseball, and steroids are just one aspect of their advantage. The NFL understood what baseball did not: the real steroid problem is the problem of public perception. If the fans are turned off by your game, you have a problem that needs to be addressed. When football fans began to question the huge bodies of its players, the NFL quickly addressed the problem through mandatory steroid testing. Lacking the will and organizational structure, baseball waited too long to do the same. Where baseball is a collection of thirty teams, the NFL is one league.

Of course, as wide as the gulf may be between the NFL's steroid policy and baseball's, that doesn't mean the NFL's steroid testing policy is especially stringent. There's an even bigger discrepancy between the NFL and the International Olympic Committee. If David Boston were an Olympian, he wouldn't have missed four weeks for a first positive test; he would have missed two years. A second offense wouldn't mean a ban of six weeks, it would mean lifetime banishment. USA Track and Field has considered implementing lifetime bans for even a first steroid offense. Most track athletes say they support the idea, yet track athletes seem to be among the biggest offenders. It was a track coach who partnered with Victor Conte, and another track coach who turned them both in.

The BALCO case may ultimately be known for what it does to the reputation of Barry Bonds. Few remember that the first introduction many had to the company was in 2003, when Bill Romanowski of the Oakland Raiders promoted its zinc pills at the Super Bowl. Later that year Romanowski and three of his teammates, defensive tackle Dana Stubblefield, center Barret Robbins, and defensive tackle Chris Cooper, tested positive for THG, also known as the "clear."

When the NFL learned about the existence of THG, many people thought its use was widespread throughout football because the NFL's tests would not detect it. The league then retested thousands of samples it had in storage and found only those four Raiders who came up positive. If the Raiders had defeated the Tampa Bay Buccaneers in Super Bowl XXXVII, would commentators call the Raiders' title tainted in the same way so many now question the home run exploits of Barry Bonds?

As the NFL worked to cleanse itself of steroids, many players began to take over-the-counter supplements to boost energy or build muscle. Many of the supplements also contained substances banned by the league. The Minnesota Vikings offensive tackle Korey Stringer died during training camp in 2001, and while there's no evidence that he used steroids, there were reports that he had ephedra bottles in his locker. The league added ephedra to its banned list that year.

Some players who have tested positive for banned substances have said they took only over-the-counter supplements that must have had something in them that was against the rules. Chicago Bears quarterback Jim Miller, who, judging by his physique, would be one of the last players suspected of using steroids, tested positive after taking what he said was an over-the-counter supplement. During the 2004 season the NFL and its players' union began a program of inspecting supplements and giving a seal of approval to those that met the league's rigorous standards. Experimental and Applied Sciences, better known as EAS, became the first supplement maker certified by the league after NSF International, a nonprofit organization that studies health and safety standards, confirmed that several products in the EAS Myoplex line met the NFL's standards. Those standards included formula evaluation, production and packaging facilities that had controls in place to avoid cross-contamination with banned substances, and clinical testing to determine if any ingredients metabolize into banned substances.

Even though the NFL has certified the supplements, the league is careful not to appear to endorse the use of supplements. The certification label on the Myoplex products specifies that the NFL and the NFL Players' Association do not endorse or encourage using supplements. The NFL doesn't put its logo on the products and doesn't receive sponsorship money from EAS. EAS is, however, loudly promoting the fact that its supplements are NFL Approved.

Unlike baseball, football's most popular players play at a position that would not greatly benefit from steroids. Quarterbacks are the league's biggest stars, and while having a stronger throwing arm or an ability to avoid pass rushers more quickly is nice, the most important part of a quarterback's game is his ability to recognize defenses and throw with accuracy. If we found out that Peyton Manning's forty-nine-touchdown season was fueled by steroids (the unlikeliest of possibilities), there might not be as much public outcry as there has been over Bonds because Manning's skills aren't perceived as depending on physical strength.

It's fair to say that the football players who would gain most from steroids would not be recognized by most of the public. But the use of other performance-enhancers—legal creatine and nitrous boosters, illegal amphetamines—and recreational drugs (most famously illustrated by former first-round pick Ricky Williams, who left the game so that he could smoke marijuana freely) show that the NFL's drug policy still has some holes.

"Serious sport," George Orwell once wrote, "has nothing to do with fair play." Steroids haven't become a scandal in football as they have in baseball not because the players by their nature are any more rule-abiding, but because of differences in structure and perception. Baseball can certainly learn from its counterpart on this issue, even if it learns only PR skills.

9

Pre-trial Commotion: The Legal Issues of Steroids and Sports

IT'S AXIOMATIC AMONG trial attorneys that most jurors make up their minds about a case not long after the lawyers have presented their opening statements. We're not making a value judgment here, we're just reporting the social science. First impressions matter a great deal, in a criminal case as in any other interpersonal relationship.

The public's reaction to high-profile criminal cases is a lot like being on a jury. When a celebrity trial makes headlines, people's minds are cast in favor of the defendant or the government almost as soon as the initial allegations become public information. The O. J. Simpson case polarized the public from the beginning. As we watched the Bronco chase, we either said, "Go, Juice, Go," or we thought he was lamming it.

As we have seen over the past several years, the public airing of the evidence against Simpson has changed very few minds. The jurors themselves sat through months of evidence, but they had made up their minds soon after the trial began. Likewise, the public's reaction to the prosecution of Martha Stewart had little to do with her guilt. People were much more concerned about the selective prosecution of celebrities than they were with the legal issues of insider trading and obstruction of justice. As often as not, what matters is not whether the dude did it, but whether we really care.

It's the same with the BALCO case. At this writing the *United States v. Conte, et al.*, as it is properly referred to, hasn't gotten as far as opening statements, but that hasn't stopped media and fans alike from rushing to judgment against the government or against the defendants. The government is on another witch-hunt; our players need to know this isn't the Soviet Union, and we don't cheat. Again, as with the Simpson and Stewart cases, our reactions to the headlines in the BALCO case tell us more about ourselves than about the merits of the prosecution's allegations.

For many of us, the law is beside the point. Lawyers and judges weigh down trials with rules of evidence and procedure, and the jury is hectored with instructions as to what they can and can't consider. But jury verdicts are rarely inconsistent with what the jurors initially believe about a case. The rules and instructions, perhaps even the statutes, may be beside the point. This doesn't mean we're necessarily wrong in jumping to conclusions— Malcolm Gladwell's *Blink* tells us that social science sees validity in snap judgments. But it does mean that when we try to discuss the merits of a legal case, we're probably not being as fair to the other side as we should be.

The goal in this chapter is to bring a degree of objectivity and a degree of fairness to discussion of the BALCO case. We'll address some of the most often-asked questions about the case, pulling these questions from media reports and selected internet sites. In choosing these questions, we'll reveal some of our own biases, but we have to start, and stop, somewhere.

There's no claim to definitiveness here. Few things in the law are plain, and definitive answers are hard to come by. We will try to avoid any attempt to weigh in on public policy. We will not address whether performance-enhancing substances should be prohibited, either in law or in a sport's governing rules. We will not discuss whether we think baseball players have been using illegal substances or whether these substances actually improve performance. Nor does this chapter purport to be an expert's view of steroid law. Anyone interested in hearing from an expert on that subject should pick up Rick Collins's book *Legal Muscle*. As you'll see in our interview with him later in this book, Collins knows more about steroid law than most people will ever need to learn. What we will try to do is establish some foundation for a discussion of the BALCO case and other similar cases that may follow in its wake.

In the preparation of this chapter, Pat Cotter, a white-collar criminal defense attorney with Arnstein & Lehr in Chicago, was an invaluable resource. Pat has spent time teaching federal criminal law to law students, and as an assistant United States attorney. He was one of the prosecutors who put John Gotti in jail.

Lawyers who read this chapter will raise sensible objections to some of what they find here. We should state again that it is not our goal to prove points in favor of the government or the defense, or to persuade anyone of what our laws should be. The goal is sobriety, not victory. For simplicity's sake, Bill James's question-and-answer format works well. With that in mind, let's get to it.

Much has been made of a Playboy *article, "Gunning for the Big Guy." Does it offer the best information about the government's case against BALCO?*

"Gunning for the Big Guy" is an intriguing, sensational article based on information from inside the investigation. It is also a flaming piece of uncorroborated hearsay. After reading the piece, one is left with the impression that the case against BALCO is nothing more than a vendetta, a shady crusade launched by one rogue IRS agent, Jeff Novitsky, who was jealous of Barry Bonds's physique and peeved at Bonds's attitude. The case, it would seem, is built on conjecture about how Bonds got so muscular and a scanty amount of evidence retrieved from a bit of dumpster diving. This might all be true. We may never know.

The article's primary source, Iran White, is not likely to be tested in court, under oath. He is no longer a law-enforcement agent. He has had a stroke and reportedly has yet to recover well enough to testify. All of this would be fertile ground for cross-examination.

Memory is always inexact. Francis Wellman's classic work, *The Art of Cross-Examination*, cites studies showing that memory may be only 75 percent accurate, and less so as time carries us away from the moment of perception. Other studies have shown that at least 10 percent of in-court testimony is demonstrably false. There are many reasons for this, including wishful thinking, preconceived notions, and sensory faults, all things that can warp one's recollections. How much would memory be distorted by a stroke? If White were called to the stand, you could bet he would spend days there, under unrelenting cross-examination.

According to *Playboy*, "To White, Novitzky—who did not participate in this article—*seemed* to have an *unusual interest* in the ballplayer." I have emphasized the words that would require some scrutiny. What, exactly, was White's basis for drawing these inferences? Can anyone corroborate this judgment under oath?

His bias would be tested too. His story was not volunteered in the interests of justice. He sold it. And given that he sold it to *Playboy*, would he have any motive to juice up the details? To make the story more salacious? He'd have to answer those questions.

There has been public concern over the veracity of the affidavit that IRS agent Jeff Novitzky filed in support of search warrants. Until the case is tried in court, we'll have no basis for determining whether the affidavit is true, but there is a fundamental difference between the affidavit and the story White sold to *Playboy*. Like White, Novitzky has not been subjected to cross-examination. Unlike White, Novitzky's version of events has been given under oath. He is subject to legal and disciplinary consequences if he is proven to have lied or otherwise fudged details of his story. All other things being equal, Noviztky's untested version is more credible than White's.

Is Playboy *right when it says, "Combining federal, state, and local authorities, the* BALCO *investigation was unprecedented in size and scope."*

Many, if not most, federal cases fall within more than one jurisdiction, so there's nothing about this case that seems atypical.

Playboy *also says, "Cracking down on* BALCO *just for money laundering would never merit such energy from law enforcement." Is that true?*

No.

Is the case against Conte and the others little more than a vendetta of one IRS agent who didn't like Barry Bonds?

Novitzky might have suspected Bonds was on steroids. He might have been irrationally envious of Bonds's physique. He might have thought Bonds was a jerk. He might have relished the idea that Bonds's reputation would suffer if BALCO were brought low. Even if that's all true, there's much more to the story.

Although the *Playboy* piece leaves the impression that the government's case, at least before the warrants were executed, amounted to nothing more than Novitzky's animus, the affidavit demonstrates there's a lot more to the case than that. Subpoenaed emails, subpoenaed trash, information from confidential informants—the tangible evidence cited in the affidavit is more than enough for the warrant to pass the smell test.

It's hard to imagine a supervisor with the IRS, or with the U.S. attorney's office, who would allow an agent to open and pursue a case based solely on what we see in the *Playboy* piece. It's hard to imagine a high-profile prosecution being brought on a case as flimsy as the one presented there. When the trial happens, we should expect to learn that there was a lot more going on than what it seemed to Iran White.

The prosecution itself would not have been initiated without substantial oversight. One of the first stages of a federal prosecution is what's called the prosecutor's memo, or proof analysis. A memo like that would address every element of every crime alleged against every defendant. All of the testimonial and tangible evidence (documents, lab materials, etc.) would be analyzed for credibility, vulnerability, and admissibility. All anticipated objections would be addressed. The memo would include case law supporting the prosecution's theories.

As Pat Cotter notes, "All that material goes to their local bosses and then, after inevitable tweaking, on to several layers of review in Washington. All of this takes time, and the bigger or more newsworthy a case, the more time it takes to get approval." This is especially true in newsworthy cases because the Department of Justice doesn't want to risk embarrassment, and it understands that high-profile defendants employ highly qualified trial attorneys. The better the defense attorneys, the greater the risk to the government.

This vetting process explains why the federal government wins almost all its cases. The feds don't attack unless they are sure they'll win. Which makes it highly unlikely that we have seen the entirety of the government's case and unthinkable that the government's case is built on a foundation as rickety as what you see in *Playboy.*

Is the investigation tainted by Novitkzy's animus toward Bonds, or by his book deal?
As we write, we don't know that he has a book deal. There are strong rumors to that effect, and so for the sake of argument we can address it as a hypothetical: would an investigation and prosecution be compromised if the lead agent sold his story before the case is finished?

The short answer is no. There's no such legal concept as "taint." Did Novitzky violate the defendants' constitutional rights during his collection of evidence? If not, the evidence can be used in court. That said, his credibility can be attacked on cross-examination. Defense attorneys can try to make something of his bias. They can hope to inflame the jury with it.

All that really matters is whether his investigation was compromised by self-interest. Unless he had the deal in place before he launched his investigation, it will be hard to make that case. If you're the cop who catches the Unabomber, should we throw out all your evidence because you signed a book deal as you were escorting Kaczynski to the jailhouse? This is more of an issue for Novitzky's supervisors than for the court.

Questions about Novitzky "tainting the case" recall the role of detective Mark Fuhrman in the O. J. Simpson criminal trial. It raises a good point about prosecutions in general. In criminal law there is no such thing as "taint." Something is either constitutional or it isn't. The motives of the investigators are largely irrelevant. If a cop hates pedophilia, does that make his investigation of a suspected pedophile unreliable? Does it mean, by itself, that the cop has violated the suspect's rights? The personal feelings of the investigators are beside the point. What matters is whether the suspect's rights were honored, and whether the evidence collected is admissible in court.

Another question has been whether the presence of U.S. Anti-Doping Agency representatives at the search of BALCO's facility taints the investigation. The argument is that only law-enforcement personnel should execute a warrant, and since the USADA is not a law-enforcement agency, its representatives should not have been on hand to assist the police. The answer is that it is not uncommon for the police to use people outside of law enforcement to assist with an investigation, search, or arrest.

It could be as simple as the cops bringing the victim over to a suspect and asking, "Is this the guy who hit you?" The victim's presence doesn't diminish the quality of the investigation. It's common in corporate cases, when private entities contact the U.S. attorney's office to let them know a private investigation has uncovered crimes. The U.S attorney could rely on that information and often will tell private investigators to continue their work and keep the government apprised. In the BALCO case, the presence of the USADA was likely nothing more sinister than an attempt by investigators to receive expert advice on what they were likely to find at the site, and to help maintain that evidence. The defense attorneys are entitled to cross-examine the government agents on any ways the USADA could have corrupted the search, but the presence of noncops does not by itself make a search unconstitutional.

Did Victor Conte, BALCO founder, and Greg Anderson, Bonds's personal trainer, confess to Novitzky?

A lot rides on the answer to this question. Novitzky's affidavit supplies highly incriminating statements allegedly made by both Conte and Anderson. There hasn't been much mention of these statements in the press, but if they're accurate they pretty much end the question of whether these men are guilty.

A statement by the suspect is not the same thing as a confession. The police define confession broadly; defense attorneys define it narrowly. "Confession" is a concept subject to various interpretations, but it has precise legal requirements. One of those requirements is that if the police place a suspect in custody and interrogate him, they must read him his rights before the interrogation begins. If they don't, and the suspect incriminates himself, prosecutors will not be able to use the statement—the confession—in court. This explanation is a bit simplified, but essentially it's accurate. You have a right *not* to tell the cops something they can use against you, and the cops have to let you know you have that right.

What happened in this case is that the investigators did not read the suspects their rights. All sides agree on this. Where they disagree is whether the suspects were in custody during the interrogation.

"Custody," like "confession," is a term of art. What it means is that a person in that situation would not have felt free to leave. According to the defense, the police raided BALCO and directed the employees where and how to sit. When someone got up, one of the police barked at her and ordered her to sit. Under those circumstances, would you feel free to leave? The government gives a different version of events, with the most notable difference being that they told the suspects they were not under arrest and were free to leave at any time. The story is more or less the same for the search of Anderson's residence.

Whether Conte and Anderson were in custody when they made statements is an issue that the court hasn't yet resolved. A lot rides on this issue because the statements, if accurately reported, are deadly to the defense. They're the kinds of statements that make a defense lawyer want to strangle his client. The judge's ruling may depend on how tolerant the court is of the police's craftiness in technically satisfying the legal requirements of a custodial interrogation. Are the police being too clever by half when they tell a suspect he can leave—but indicate by their actions that he cannot?

Is the case against BALCO really a case against Barry Bonds?

Bonds's attorney, Michael Rains, says it is. Rains has been quoted as saying, "My view has always been this case has been the *U.S. v. Bonds*, and I think the government has moved in certain ways in a concerted effort to indict my client." Rains is not the only one saying it. An article appeared in *Reason* magazine—"*Bush v. Bonds*"—alleging that Bonds is the prime target of the BALCO investigation.

Greg Gagne, a colleague and not the former shortstop, answers the question this way:

> This BALCO place really isn't all about Bonds, or even all about baseball players; track and field folks would scoff at the idea that this whole thing revolves around baseball. Not to mention [Bill] Romanowski, who retired shortly after this story hit the streets. This was a high-scale drug operation, and the only reason Conte isn't hanging from the rafters already is because his clients were famous. If he were shooting up the local high school football team, parents would burn him at the stake.

The evidence that has been made public backs up Greg, not Mr. Rains. Incidentally, wasn't it a track and field coach that kicked the case into high gear?

Bonds does make for a good straw man. I can't fault Rains for trying to rehabilitate his client's image, but I have to ask, what would Bonds be indicted for? Even if you assume Bonds took steroids intentionally and knew what he was doing, it's not clear he committed any crime. He might have, but the government would have a hard time proving it.

Why? For one thing, the Controlled Substances Act (from this point on, simply "the Act") does not expressly prohibit drug *use*. Drug use is a crime in certain circumstances, such as while one is a member of the military service, but it's not a crime per se under federal law. If that surprises you, you're not alone. I spoke with an assistant United States attorney who prosecutes drug cases for a living, and he didn't know that the Act does not criminalize drug use.

But it doesn't. You can look it up.

In fact, check the state laws against controlled substances and you won't find many that criminalize use. When we asked Rick Collins about this, he had to think a moment and then said, "Arizona makes a distinction between use and possession. Off the top of my head, I can't think of any others that do. It's exceedingly rare to criminalize use, and this isn't an unintentional oversight. Our drug laws have always focused on possession and sale, not use."

Consider the case of Rush Limbaugh. He used a staggering amount of controlled substances, but he is not being prosecuted for drug use. Florida is prosecuting him for doctor shopping by invoking a rarely used statute.

If the principal aim of the Act is to keep unsafe drugs out of the hands of people who aren't qualified to use them, this implies that the users are victims of a predatory black market or of negligent doctors and pharmacologists. If that's true, it makes sense not to criminalize use. This is not to say that use shouldn't be criminalized; it's to say that if we read the Act to criminalize use, we are being hypocritical and illogical.

This hasn't stopped some courts from inferring that use is subsumed by the proscription against drug possession. Most federal courts that have looked at this issue have found that a prosecution for possession based on drug use is valid. Presence of the drug inside the body—discovered by a positive result on a valid drug test—does not mean for sure that the defendant possessed it, but it usually does. The courts reason that if a drug makes its way inside a person, it is logical to assume the person had to possess it, however briefly, before consuming it. If a person says he ate a hamburger for lunch, you can safely assume he held it in his hands before eating it.

Even if a federal prosecutor could sustain a case for use, you won't find one that would bother. The actual charge would be for simple possession, a very low-level misdemeanor. Under the Act, the number of pills or amount of liquid that qualifies as a single dose of steroids is huge. For example, fifty pills are considered to be one dose. The penalty for this kind of possession would be small; it wouldn't be worth the time of a U.S. attorney's office to prosecute. As Pat Cotter notes, "The next time I see a federal prosecution for use alone, it will be the first time. Simple possession is dealt out to the states. The best example is at airports where feds regularly turn over small drug cases to state authorities."

Is it feasible that the U.S. attorney would build a case around Barry Bonds, knowing that at worst he committed the lowest-level offense? Why would the prosecutors waste their time, and risk enormous embarrassment, when they have solid evidence against at least four suspects—the four men actually being tried in *United States v. Conte, et al*?

Why do lawyers talk to the media?
They shouldn't, but they do. It's usually the criminal defense attorneys who do the talking. Prosecutors have ethical rules that restrict their freedom to make "extrajudicial" statements. You'll occasionally see a prosecutor say more than "no comment," but it won't be much more. We expect our prosecutors to be above the fray.

Why shouldn't criminal defense attorneys talk to the media? Public relations is a field of expertise unto itself, and lawyers aren't trained in PR. A more important reason is credibility. Credibility is sometimes a criminal defense attorney's only weapon. As a defense attorney you are allowed, when representing your client in court, to make arguments that don't necessarily square with the truth. This can charitably be called zealous advocacy. When you do it outside of a courtroom, it's called lying. When you lie, you lose credibility.

Sometimes an attorney has no choice. Sometimes a client demands his attorney say something before his reputation is irreparably damaged. So the attorney says something. He could say, "My client is, if anything, a victim in this case." It's something banal but assertive. There's no need to talk about Masonic plots to destroy your client.

In court, though, outrageous stories can be useful. Sometimes wild stories are the only way to create reasonable doubt. If a jury likes the client—or if they are charmed by the attorney—the jury may go to the ends of the earth to deliver an acquittal by finding that doubt.

If the BALCO cases don't all end up in guilty pleas—at least some of them will—the defense attorneys will probably stick to the defenses we have been discussing here. These aren't the kinds of arguments you'd make to a judge, but you might with a jury. They're not likely to win, but with a jury you never know what can happen.

Why isn't the government going after whoever it was that leaked the players' grand jury testimony?
They *are* investigating the leak. The government seized Conte's computer as part of their investigation. That doesn't mean he's the source, but it does show they're looking into it. It's far too

early to say the government has swept this one under the carpet. It is true, though, that leaks in most cases are from the government itself—someone in the prosecutor's office who got access to the grand jury transcripts and wanted to feel like a big shot. The press is very good at conning information out of people, and it's easy to believe that many people on the government's side might be tempted to tell what they heard around the water cooler. But for all we know, the defense was the source of the leak. It's just too soon to talk much about this.

It is important to note that despite recent cases against journalists, the First Amendment still protects the rights of the press. Mark Fainaru-Wada and the investigative team at the *San Francisco Chronicle* had every right to publish the testimony in their stories, even if the person that gave it to them was committing a crime.

If the government leaked Barry Bonds's grand jury testimony, did they violate his right to privacy?

Not necessarily. First, it has nothing to do with Bonds's right to privacy. What's at issue here is that the proceedings of the grand jury are not to be disclosed except under limited circumstances. Grand jury proceedings are kept secret for strategic reasons, not to protect civil liberties.

In the case of *Douglas Oil v. Petrol Stops Northwest,* the Supreme Court gave five reasons for grand jury secrecy:

(1) To prevent the escape of those whose indictment may be contemplated; (2) to insure the utmost freedom to the grand jury in its deliberations, and to prevent persons subject to indictment or their friends from importuning the grand jurors; (3) to prevent subornation of perjury or tampering with the witness who may testify before [the] grand jury and later appear at

the trial of those indicted by it; (4) to encourage free and un-trammeled disclosures by persons who have information with respect to the commission of crimes; (5) to protect innocent accused who is exonerated from disclosure of the fact that he has been under investigation, and from the expense of standing trial where there was no probability of guilt.

In short, we don't want to tip off the bad guys that we're on to them, and we don't want the bad guys to get to the witnesses. Bonds was, by all published accounts, a reluctant witness. He did not wish to give free and untrammeled testimony. The justifications for keeping grand jury testimony secret do not seem to apply to Bonds.

But let's make this point clear: there is no excuse for leaking Bonds's testimony. The person who did that ought to be investigated. Yet people go too far when they allege that Bonds was betrayed by the system or that the gravest injustice in the BALCO case is the leak of the players' testimony.

What could change this view is evidence that the prosecutors intentionally leaked the testimony in an effort to humiliate the athletes. Absent evidence of that, it looks like an unfortunate incident that doesn't really have any bearing on the case.

Bonds says he didn't know exactly what he was using. Is that a defense?
He isn't going to be prosecuted, so this is an academic question.

If one reads the excerpts from his grand jury testimony, they actually make Bonds look better, not worse, than he looked before the leaks appeared. They make him sound like he had no idea he was using a controlled substance. In a case like this, the prosecution would have to show that the defendant knew what he was using.

He says he didn't know, but the follow-up question is whether he *should* have known. In a drug case the prosecution can get the judge to give the jury what's called an "ostrich" instruction. It's also called "deliberate avoidance." If the defendant had reason to suspect that what he was using (or possessing) was a controlled substance, but he deliberately avoided finding out what it was—in other words, if he put his head in the sand—he can be found guilty. It would come down to whether the jury believes him.

Reportedly Bonds said he didn't know it was a steroid, and he says he used it on his joints. Proper usage of the drug, as evidenced by the instructions on the Androgel website, tells me that you wouldn't use testosterone on your joints if you knew what you were doing and wanted full effect. This suggests Bonds is telling the truth—but it also sounds conveniently legalistic. It's hard to fathom why Anderson, in light of their close relationship, wouldn't have told him how to use it properly unless there was an understanding of "don't ask, don't tell" between the athlete and his personal trainer.

Is it significant that Barry Bonds received immunity to testify before the grand jury?

It could mean that he's not a target at all, let alone the prime target.

Bonds was given transactional immunity. This means that his testimony cannot be used as evidence against him if he is eventually prosecuted. This raises an added concern for the prosecutor: before securing the grant of immunity, he should have documented what he intends to prosecute Bonds for, if anything. This helps him avoid the appearance of bad faith later.

Here's an example. Say a client is being prosecuted for possessing marijuana. Before we get our case to court, the prosecution immunizes him and compels him to testify against his friend, who is the dealer. During the testimony, the client reveals that he has sold mushrooms. The government will have a problem if they add a charge for selling mushrooms. Unless they can show that the evidence supporting the change was derived independently of his testimony, they would probably be prohibited from prosecuting him for dealing mushrooms. The best way to make sure that doesn't happen is to document what the plan is before the grant of immunity. If something else comes out, that's the cost of doing business; let it go.

Apply this to Bonds's case. If he was the big fish, why immunize him at all? Consider that the prosecution would have to have had all their evidence against him lined up before granting the immunity. Since none of the BALCO defendants has been prosecuted yet, why would they give a grant to Bonds so early, if in fact Bonds is the prime target? Maybe this is too simplistic an argument, but it looks clear from the immunity deal (and other good reasons) that Bonds was collateral damage; he was not a prime target.

Did the government, knowing it had no case against Barry Bonds for steroids, try to get him by setting a "perjury trap"?

They would be stupid if they tried. You can't really set someone up for perjury. All Bonds would have to do to avoid the trap would be to tell the truth.

To prove Bonds lied about his possession or use of steroids, prosecutors would have to show that he in fact knowingly used them. If they could prove that, they wouldn't need to set a perjury trap.

Why didn't the FBI go after the players in the 1990s?

For the same reason they don't go after users now. Users are victims, and prosecutions for simple possession are usually not worth the effort. Our public policy is to hit those higher on the food chain.

Why hasn't the government gone after the big fish?

In this case, the "big fish" often means the actual creators of the performance-enhancing substances, the chemists. BALCO is a link down the food chain from the guys we're talking about. There has been a great deal of speculation about this, including some names. There have been media reports indicating that the feds have been investigating this line, so the more precise question might be why the government hasn't initiated a prosecution against the creators.

The straightest answer is that they may still be building their case. The prosecution may be hoping that Conte and the other BALCO defendants will help them work their way up to the top of the chain. It's also possible that some have worked out a deal with the government.

What underlies this question is the insinuation that the government really isn't after the big fish, that this case upends the traditional prosecutorial scheme: instead of focusing on the kingpin, they're targeting the users. The problem with this argument is that no user has been indicted and none is likely to be indicted. The government is prosecuting those involved in manufacturing, distribution, and substantial possession. By all appearances, this is a standard prosecution.

Assume one of these big fish has cut a deal with the government and is working as a confidential informant. Assume he has convinced baseball players that his new drug is undetectable. Assume they take it. Now, assume the drug is readily detectable and that the players get caught. In other words, he set them up. Would this be entrapment because he was working for the government?

Probably not. There isn't a universal legal definition of entrapment, but one thing the defense would have to show is that the players were not predisposed to break the law. If the big fish came to them and offered the drug and they said no, only to give in after being pestered, it could very well be entrapment. If the athletes merely responded to an offer of drugs, no. We're brought back to the question of whether the federal government would expend that much effort on simple possession.

Should the government be able to use the results of baseball's drug tests, even though MLB promised the union in collective bargaining that the testing would protect anonymity?

Yes. Personal agreements cannot provide immunities to legal process for the people who manage to arrange them. In other words, the law applies to everyone, even professional athletes who have a union that successfully negotiates some privacy protection for them vis-à-vis a transaction with the league.

The same sort of situation could be imagined with a landlord: he and I agree that what I do in my apartment is completely private, and I specifically tell him to admit no one. Surely no one would argue that the police could not use evidence of a crime (drugs, murder, counterfeiting, child pornography) that they found in my apartment after a search pursuant to a warrant simply because I had an agreement with my landlord not to let anyone in.

Also, it makes no sense that an agreement between two individuals (players and the league) can limit the otherwise legal rights of a third party (the government), which was not a party to the agreement.

BALCO is being prosecuted for mislabeling THG, but other companies sold other compounds that were like THG and were also mislabeled. Why aren't the feds going after them?

We don't know they aren't. We only know about BALCO because it's a high-profile case. Even if the government isn't going after those other companies, it's not a legitimate defense. Every criminal defense attorney has to make this point to a client at some time. It's like getting busted with your hand in the cookie jar. "Johnny took a cookie too, and you didn't do anything to him!" It didn't work with your mother when you were four years old, and it won't work in criminal court. Selective prosecution is a policy issue, not a defense.

First Martha, now Barry. Why are we persecuting celebrities?

The government is damned if it does and damned if it doesn't. Prosecute the little guy and people will complain that the celebrities are getting off light because of their fame. Prosecute celebrities and you're doing it to make yourself famous.

A case can be made for selective prosecution. The government doesn't have the resources to go after everyone it suspects of criminal activity. Given a choice, does it go after the little guy, or does it go after the celebrity? If it goes after the celebrity, it will make an example of her, but that's not necessarily a bad thing. A prosecution like that can have substantial value as public education. The Martha Stewart prosecution brought a lot of attention to insider trading and obstruction of justice. The prosecution of BALCO has already brought a lot of attention to steroids.

These prosecutions do more than educate the public about crimes and the consequences of violating those crimes. By bringing the issues to the forefront of news coverage, they provoke debate over public policy and can prompt those policies to be changed and made more just.

At least celebrities can afford the best attorneys.

Is George W. Bush coordinating the persecution of ballplayers?

The argument runs like this: Bush is using the Justice Department to drag the players through the mud, because it's his way of getting revenge against Bud Selig for not making him Commissioner of Baseball more than a decade ago.

This isn't a question directly related to the legal case against the BALCO defendants, but it does allege prosecutorial misconduct of a sort. In the military it would be called "unlawful command influence." Prosecutors have an ethical obligation under their rules of professional conduct not to prosecute a case unless they are convinced there is probable cause that the defendant committed the crime. They don't need to be convinced beyond a reasonable doubt, but they do have to believe the case is legitimate. If the prosecutors are merely following orders and selectively prosecuting people they don't believe are guilty, but are doing it because their boss wants to settle a score with some nonparty, they would be committing grave ethical violations. The problem with the theory is that there is substantial evidence of the defendants' guilt and no published evidence that the president was involved in any way with Novitzky's investigation.

What this sounds like to me is what psychologists call "over-inclusive thinking." That's when a person takes data from a variety of sources and then contorts the data so that it fits his preconceptions. It's common to those who thrive on conspiracy theories. The data involved here:

—George W. Bush was involved in baseball.
—He wanted to be commissioner.
—He was denied the chance to be commissioner.
—He became president.
—Baseball's best player is caught up in a steroid scandal.
—Bush, as president, is now in a position to get revenge.
—Bush can use the Justice Department and its prosecutors to exact that revenge.

Milder forms of this conspiracy theory can be found all over the internet and in the print media. Overinclusive thinkers need to stretch the data in their lives or else they can't make sense of the world. What's obvious to you is not obvious to them. Suggest to them that the president is pandering by hitching a ride on a kosher prosecution and they won't buy it. Occam's Razor cuts nothing here.

Overinclusive thinking is common among people who see authority figures as malevolent. There is no doubt that many people in the United States view George W. Bush as a malevolent force. Often these are the same people who alternatively figure Bush for a dunce and a mastermind. The question isn't a serious legal question. It might be a serious question for social scientists.

10

Profile: The Student

"I CAN REMEMBER exactly when I first thought about this," Wes told me, setting the glass vial on the table and removing a syringe from its protective wrapper. He drew the dose precisely while he talked, looking far too expert. "I was at the tournament in Phoenix, and after I'd pitched, we were walking out and there were a bunch of scouts. I guess that's the whole purpose, right? To be seen by the scouts?"

He slid the needle into his upper thigh with only a small wince, pushing the plunger and watching the clear substance go into his muscle. "This one old guy asked me where I was from and then how tall my dad was. That was one I'd never heard before."

"How tall were you at the time?" I asked him.

"I'm not sure. Maybe five-eight?"

"And this was when?"

"Two years ago." He paused, putting the syringe into a small red plastic container. "I told him that Dad was a bit taller than me. He's—what, five-eleven? How tall are you, Will?"

"My driver's license says six foot. I'm really five-ten."

"What, are you trying to get drafted too?" Lying on a driver's license suddenly seemed quite tame. "Anyway, I tell the guy this, and he literally crosses my name off a list. He tells me, 'Call me if you hit six-two' and walks off." Somehow Wes understood how ridiculous the remark was, yet it would change his life in ways that we still don't know. "I came home and that was all I could think about. I could pitch as good as I could, and if I wasn't tall, that didn't matter?"

It was a bias of baseball men for ages. Pitchers, like anyone, fit a type. They were tall, thick, and had powerful legs. In looking for the next Curt Schilling, they wanted the possibilities to look like Curt Schilling. I've heard several scouts half-joke about cloning putting them out of a job.

Wes doesn't look like Curt Schilling. He looks more like an average teenager, skinny with traces of acne. He carries a backpack all the time, filled with notebooks, his beloved iPod, and, in a small plastic case, his vial of Seristim. This healthy, normal teenager is regularly taking a form of human growth hormone.

Also known as Geref, the drug that Wes takes several times a day is normally prescribed for children who have low hormone levels, resulting in small stature. This is, essentially, a drug that grows people. In modern society it could be considered very difficult to live at a severe disadvantage in height. Not only would it affect activities like driving and using equipment designed for average-sized persons, but some findings indicate that tall people have important social advantages.

But Geref and other, similar drugs are intended for children who are facing life at less than five feet tall. A chemical booster that brings them to five-one or five-two as adults, while still below the average height for American males, would provide a quantum change in their quality of life. Wes, on the other hand, and thousands of others are in no uncertain terms abusing this drug.

Wes is at no disadvantage. He's athletic, popular, and healthy. He's a good-looking kid, perhaps not a model, but he always seems to have friends and girls around when he's not playing baseball or basketball. At sixteen and a junior at a large suburban high school, he's nearly the definition of normal. Picture his disheveled hair, Abercrombie & Fitch clothes, and Dodge truck as just extensions of himself. His grades are above average, mostly As and Bs, but he'll admit that he doesn't apply himself as he could. He's never had any trouble with the law or even with his parents beyond the norm. He even occasionally says please and thank you.

To me the biggest surprise was not that Wes would take this drug. He wants more than anything else to be a professional athlete. He's seen his father, a manager at a local manufacturer, leave for work each morning and come home each evening for the last sixteen years. The family lives in a nice home in a pleasant subdivision. His father takes him to Pacers games, good seats in the lower level that they've had since Wes was old enough to go. The surprise was that his parents would go along with his drug taking.

Wes's father had dreams of being an athlete himself. He's always made sure that Wes had everything he would need, from a basketball goal at the end of the driveway to top-of-the-line Nike Shox shoes. Wes's truck is new—not the best, perhaps, but better than most kids have at sixteen. He's taken lessons, both baseball and basketball, since he began playing. Anytime there's a suggestion made, his father has a habit of asking, "Is it the best for him?"

When Wes first came to me almost a year ago for pitching lessons, I wondered if a kid like him would work hard. Things seemed to come a little too easy for him. In our first session together, he was able to make some minor but difficult changes to his stride without altering anything else. It was the same when he learned a new changeup and even a breaking ball.

What wouldn't come easy was getting that scout's throwaway remark out of his mind. He knew—and his father knew—that he could be the best pitcher, with the best glove and cleats, and it might not matter. Lessons, curveballs, results—it might all go for naught if the scout saw him at eighteen and said "too short." Somehow scouts ignored their own trained eyes on things like this. Greg Maddux, Roy Oswalt, Billy Wagner, and others have all put up excellent numbers, winning or challenging for Cy Young awards and ERA titles. All are under six feet tall, well under in some cases.

Wes's mother knew someone who'd taken growth hormone as an anti-aging measure, and she made a couple of calls. It wasn't hard to find a doctor willing to prescribe the hormone, despite Wes giving every appearance of being a normal, healthy, average-sized teenager. Once the doctor wrote the prescription, the real decision had to be made. The drug is not cheap, running just under $1,000 a month, not including the medical tests required while taking it. Even for this well-to-do family, that's a significant expense.

Wes's mother seemed surprised when I asked to talk with her about this issue. After she decided to try to obtain growth hormone for Wes, she seems to have instantly shifted her thinking to the position that this was completely normal. Only occasionally are there cracks in this veneer, when her maternal instincts break through with worries about later effects on Wes.

"We didn't do this just because of baseball," she said, looking more at her coffee than at me. "Some of the doctors we talked to actually said the injections might do more for me or his father than for Wes. There's a lot of research they showed us about anti-aging, but it really made me feel better that a doctor would be monitoring this. I wish we could use the Lilly product since they're right here [in Indianapolis], but really, it's trusting the doctors that watch out for Wes."

"If it hadn't been for baseball, would you have considered this?" I asked.

She paused. "No, I guess not. Maybe for basketball."

There are cracks in the veneer of this perfect family. They live in the suburbs, perhaps the last of the families you might mistake for the Cleavers. Their daughter, a few years younger than Wes, also plays sports.

"What if your daughter needs something similar?"

Both parents looked at each other. I've caught them unawares, considering something that, inexplicably, had never occurred to them. "But she's fine," Wes Sr. says, as if something's not fine with his son.

Wes doesn't think of the injections much. They're part of the day now, like lunch or flirting with girls. Talking with him while his friends stood around was different; I was clearly the outsider, and he wasn't as open. I doubt any of his friends had seen him open the small plastic box in his backpack.

Alone again, I asked him how his friends or even his teammates dealt with his injections. "Most of them don't know," he said, not quite looking me in the eye. "I'm not going to pull them out when we're at practice. I don't know what they would think. I'm not the best guy on the team, and I'm not the worst either." He paused, looking out the window. "It's not something I think about."

"Why not?" I asked. "Is it because you don't want to?"

"No, I don't want to. You know what? I don't know whether anyone else on the team is taking something. There are steroids around here. There's some football guys I think have some, and this isn't like that. I don't know what other guys are doing and, you know, I don't care either.

"The doctors I have and the coaches all are after the same thing I am, and that's to get drafted."

"Drafted. Or college?" I mentioned the possibility that Wes might not make it. It was one of the things I know he didn't consider.

"College. . ." He could only say it in uncertain terms. "That's the fallback. Dad says that I can be whatever I want to be, and you tell me I can pitch, so that's all I'm focused on. College seems like failure, even if I go. Everybody I know goes to college, and it doesn't really get you anywhere, does it? It doesn't make you special, even if you go to a good school."

Wes often seems to be suffering a crisis of self-esteem. His identity is wrapped up in the idea of being something that he's not yet become and, frankly, is unlikely ever to be. The odds against becoming a professional pitcher, even drafted in the late rounds— something that would be unacceptable to Wes, I'm sure—are high. It's not unrealistic to think he might play college baseball, but as he says himself, that might not be enough.

Jim Andrews, the eminent orthopedic surgeon, said recently that he often questions surgery for some players, but he usually defers to their desire to play again. "Who am I to tell them their dream is over?" he told an audience at a recent convention.

Andrews is right, as usual, but there's also a larger dynamic here. Not every pitcher, no matter how big his dream, will make the big leagues. Not all will get a scholarship or even make the varsity. The decision as to whether someone should have surgery is very similar to the decision a player must make about taking performance-enhancing drugs. Is it worth it?

"What happens later, Wes?" I asked. His normal time frame for forward thinking might range to his next meal, but this made him a bit contemplative.

"I don't think about that. I heard when the doctor told me the side effects, but that's why I have the doctor. He watches me. My parents watch me. If something happens, I'll stop."

I wondered about this. "Would you stop? Really? If you're willing to go this far—to stick needles in yourself all day—what's to say you wouldn't go just a bit further? If I tell you this stuff gets you 99 percent of the way there, I know you'd go that extra distance."

Wes nodded, his eyes distant. "I guess. It depends on what that 1 percent is. Steroids? Not if it's a risk of being caught or having my balls shrivel up. There's guys I know that take Ritalin. I haven't done that."

"Does it work?"

He nodded again. "Yeah."

Wes's room looks like most teenage boys' rooms look, or rather, what I think they would look like. He has pictures of ballplayers, photos of friends on his last trip to Florida, and stacks of magazines. His stereo and computer glow across the room. His small fridge below his desk hums quietly, filled with Gatorade, Mountain Dew, and the small plastic box where he keeps his growth hormone at night.

In the dining room, on an off-white molding that surrounds the door, there's a typical American feature: the multiple pencil marks that record a growing child. This child is sixteen, not hoping to grow up or ride the big rides but to reach some magic number. The six-foot mark is a noticeable red line.

There's a red line on the side of his syringes too. It marks where he should fill each dose before injecting it into himself.

"Do you feel any different?" I asked.

"No," he said, thinking. "I haven't noticed anything except three inches of height. The last time I went to the doctor, he thought I'd hit six foot by the time baseball season comes around. I think we'll make the tournament this year, and if not, I'll go to some of the showcases again and they'll see.

"I mean, I'll list at six foot in the program, maybe six-one. Everyone lies on that thing."

"Is it a lie to say you're six foot now, since it's the drugs—or might you have grown anyway."

"No!" he exclaimed a bit too excitedly. He was invested in these drugs. He needed them to work, because without them he had to give up the dream. Without them he was merely another teenager.

I had hoped to speak with Wes's coach, but when I found out that he didn't know Wes was using growth hormone, I decided against it. While the use of growth hormone by prescription is not technically illegal under Indiana high school rules (and those of many other states, according to the National High School Federation), it does hold an ethical dilemma for coaches. To me the question of whether to inform his coach was a decision best left to Wes and his family.

I did speak with a couple of Wes's teammates, who both knew of his usage and did not question it in the least. So I imagine the coach knows. It would be a position I would not want to be in. Wes isn't the kind of player who will single-handedly change a high school baseball game. His use of a pseudo-legal substance is an ethical dilemma for all concerned, but he's not going to "call the integrity of the game into question," as some have famously said about Barry Bonds's alleged use of performance enhancers.

Wes just wants to keep dreaming, to regain that hope that a thoughtless scout took from him. I only wish that Wes would look more at the pictures on his wall for his dreams than to a vial of growth hormone. Roy Oswalt, Greg Maddux, and Billy Wagner are pinned side by side over his desk. All are major league pitchers. All would stand under the red line in Wes's kitchen.

11

On the Horizon: Genetic Performance Enhancement

IF ANYONE remembers the BALCO scandal twenty years from now, we may hear any number of comments: "What a shame." "A dark moment in baseball history." "Barry who?" Or we may hear something else:

"How primitive."

BALCO and other doping scandals represent the state of the art in performance enhancement today, but more comprehensive, sophisticated, effective, and elusive methods are poised to invade sports. New approaches will emerge from discoveries in biomedical research, in particular from the human genome project.

Future doping methods may be able to tailor drug treatments to an individual's unique genetic complement via the science of pharmacogenomics, even introducing new, performance-enhancing genes into an athlete's body through gene therapy. The appeal to the ballplayer or any other athlete is clear: these technologies have the potential to provide athletic improvement equal to or greater than anything seen today with drugs such as steroids or EPO, but with—in theory—far fewer side effects and a greatly reduced chance of detection.

HOW TO ASSEMBLE A HUMAN BEING
(BATTERIES NOT INCLUDED)

The Human Genome Project was conceived in 1985 and 1986 as the logical and necessary next step in biomedical research. Dr. Renato Dulbecco, a Nobel Prize–winning cancer biologist and one of the first to propose the project, says that he "came to the conclusion that the only way to make progress in the field (of cancer research) was to know all the genes in the human genome." This is the first and main benefit of identifying the sequence of all three billion bits of DNA that make up the human genome: the sequence provides a fundamental component of the blueprint for a human being, the parts list.

Knowing the genome sequence gives researchers a hefty boost in systematically identifying and characterizing all the genes that contribute to growth, development, and physiology. The genome sequence is being combined with sophisticated pattern-finding computational algorithms, high-speed computers, and high-throughput experimental pipelines to identify almost every gene functioning in the human body, including many that would have been difficult to identify any other way.

This almost complete list of genes gives researchers a big step up in unraveling human biology. You might not know how to build a car from scratch, but if you had all the parts lying around the garage, you'd be a lot closer than if you'd only seen NASCAR on TV. Once the parts list is available, not only is it easier to figure out how a basic human works, you can also begin to see why humans differ from one another. Knowing that Gary Sheffield has some of the fastest wrists in baseball is one thing, but how did they get that way? The genome sequence serves as a baseline, a standard of comparison so that specific differences can be identified. Any two human beings are more than 99.9 percent identical to each other in their DNA. That 0.1 percent, though, is where things get interesting. Every car has a Model T in its genes, but it's the little differences that separate a Porsche from a minivan.

The little differences among peoples' genes are already being studied in relation to disease. As an example, some northern European populations have a relatively high proportion of people who are resistant to infection by HIV, the virus that causes AIDS. It turns out their resistance is due to a particular genetic variant in a gene called CCR-5. CCR-5 is a protein that sits on the surface of immune cells and serves as the handhold to which the HIV virus attaches during the initial phase of invasion and infection. In the resistant populations, CCR-5 is missing, meaning HIV has no way of entering the body's cells, nothing to grab hold of to start the infection process. People who lack CCR-5 are much harder—almost impossible—to infect with HIV.

Other studies have uncovered a genetic component to disease susceptibility. Heart disease, cholesterol levels, adult-onset diabetes, and some kinds of cancer have all been linked to genetic factors. A recent review in the journal *Science* listed seven genes that, when present in a specific genetic variant form, lead to a greater risk of adult-onset diabetes. In time the range of human characteristics and behaviors mapped out like this will expand to a huge catalog of predispositions and potentials, and people may be able to have their genetic propensities mapped out with a quick visit to the genetic counselor.

How might our knowledge of the human genome affect baseball? Are we looking at a future of seven-foot pitchers hurling 110-mile-per-hour fastballs at batters who rise from the batter's box like brick walls but swing and run with the speed and grace of jungle cats? Well, no. Gross changes in an athlete's physiology would require far too much tinkering in the genome to be practical for decades in the future, if ever.

Initial applications are likely to be more subtle. What seems probable instead is that, as with EPO and anabolic steroids before them, selected genetic treatments and techniques will be co-opted for off-label uses. Whether or not such treatments actually improve performance on the field, technologically savvy players will experiment upon themselves, trying to get an edge. The two genomic technologies most likely to influence baseball are pharmacogenomics and gene therapy.

DOWN ON THE PHARM

Pharmacogenomics is the study of how to tailor medicine to a person's genes. Many drugs have unfortunate side effects. A recent prominent example is Vioxx, a type of drug known as a cox-2 inhibitor. It was released to the marketplace as an inflammation and pain-relief medicine. In September 2004, Vioxx was removed from the market when reports surfaced claiming its use was linked to an increase in heart disease in some users.

Side effects like these often arise from an interaction between a drug and a specific gene variant or variants within the affected people. But what if people could be screened quickly in the doctor's office for their susceptibilities before heading out to the pharmacy? Bad reactions would be drastically reduced, and a number of drugs that could have helped a substantial fraction of the population but were shelved because of legal and health concerns would be back in circulation.

Now turn this around. Just as some gene variants predispose people to react poorly to a given drug, other gene variants lead to a better-than-average reaction to specific pharmaceuticals. A recent case study reported in the *New York Times* in January 2005 described a woman who had suffered a lack of sexual desire upon taking the anti-depressant Zoloft. When prescribed the additional anti-depressant Wellbutrin, she suddenly found herself not just regaining her sexual appetites but experiencing an orgasm that lasted, on and off, for two hours. Now that's a side effect. Eventually the known side effects of drugs, good and bad, will be correlated with specific genetic variants.

The catalog of drugs that will be characterized in this way is immense. More than four thousand drugs are currently approved for prescription sales. Clandestine laboratories also produce variants of known chemicals, such as designer steroids like tetrahydrogestrinone (THG). Biomedical researchers are discovering and describing dozens to hundreds of bioactive molecules that have dramatic biological effects. All of these are candidates for use in pharmacogenomics programs to enhance athletic performance.

Here's how it might work: Athletes and their personal medical experts would start by analyzing the genotype, or specific genetic variants, of the athlete seeking an edge. The experts would then read through the catalog of drugs and compare the list of known effects and side effects to an athlete's own genome sequence. They could pick and choose among esoteric pharmaceuticals to produce a precisely tailored physical, emotional, or mental effect. This would create a nightmare for drug testing, as one of the problems with current testing regimens is the already high number of drugs available to athletes, including some drugs not yet detectable. Developing a testing regimen for every possible drug that could have a performance-enhancing effect may be impossible. This increases the odds that an artificial enhancement will go undetected. Identifying one out of one hundred drugs is difficult; picking one out of a thousand is nearly impossible given current techniques. Pharmacogenomics offers the very real possibility that there may be millions.

In baseball, pharmacogenomics might be applied in the area of stimulants. Many recent articles about the new drug-testing policy in baseball have noted the conspicuous absence of amphetamines from the list of banned substances. Let's say, however, that at some future point baseball decides it's not in the best interest of the sport to have players amped up on greenies. Pharmacogenomics may allow a baseball player to identify amphetamines that, while not effective for most people, work well for people with his particular gene variants.

Depending upon the resources of that player, it might be possible for a chemical laboratory to take its knowledge of a player's genetic variants and synthesize a chemical derivative of a common amphetamine. That derivative would be both effective, given that player's genes, and undetectable, due to changes in the chemical structure of the drug itself. Researchers are already using this technique, called "intelligent drug design," to synthesize some drugs more efficiently and quickly.

An early example of a designed drug, released in 2001, is Gleevec. Gleevec was designed specifically to inhibit an abnormal protein, BCR-ABL, that causes chronic myelogenous leukemia (CML). As opposed to normal chemotherapy agents, which essentially attack and kill any rapidly dividing cell in the body (cancer, hair, and the intestinal lining among others), Gleevec binds and affects only BCR-ABL in CML cancer cells, leading to fewer side effects and effective treatment of the cancer. Similarly targeted and designed drugs may give athletes a tailor-made chemical edge. A drug custom designed for an athlete might never be detectable because anti-doping agencies would not even know it existed.

Pharmacogenomics poses ethical questions as well. What is the practice of sport about other than taking advantage of one's own genetic uniqueness? Unless we want to live in the world Kurt Vonnegut depicted in "Harrison Bergeron," where people who are above average get "treated" with physical restraints to bring them back down to the level of everyone else, baseball will continue to glorify that tiny percentage of us who have the underlying genetic ability to hit a tiny ball with a skinny stick really, really hard.

It's an open question where the line will be drawn between nutritional supplements of all sorts and the use of chemical and biological agents that interact synergistically with an athlete's genes. If an athlete has a gene that allows him or her to eat Twinkies and somehow turn that into solid muscle, is it fair to ban Twinkies from the fast-food aisle at the local 7-11? It's an often ignored but undeniable truth that professional athletes are already, in some very targeted ways, genetic freaks.

MAKING THE MOST OF WHAT YOU DIDN'T GET

What if all it took to gain muscle with almost no effort was a change in a single gene? In June 2004 the *New England Journal of Medicine* carried a report by Dr. Marcus Shuelke and colleagues that described a child in Germany who possessed unusually developed muscles at birth. The child completely lacks a gene, myostatin, which inhibits muscle development. He has continued to exhibit unusual muscular development throughout his first years, including the ability, at the age of four, to hold seven-pound weights in either hand with his arms extended. His mother, a former track athlete, also displays unusual musculature, which at least in part may be because she has only a single functioning copy of myostatin. Many of baseball's best athletes, such as Barry Bonds and Ken Griffey, Jr., clearly benefited from their fathers passing on "baseball genes."

Gene therapy is the name given to a variety of technologies aimed at introducing new genes into the body. In most of these technologies, genes are carried into the patient's cells using viruses. Gene therapy aims to cure a medical condition through the introduction of additional genes, or to replace or fix genes that aren't working properly. Some ongoing gene therapy trials include potential treatments for cystic fibrosis, cancer, and cardiovascular disease. The threat to sports is that some of these treatments, when applied to healthy individuals, could provide an advantage in competition.

Gene therapy holds a strong appeal for an athlete. Athletic performance is derived from the interaction between genes and environment—a player's training regimen. As differences in training regimens become smaller and smaller, it's likely that some athletes will look to the other component of the performance equation for an edge. What's more, the introduction of genes can, in many cases, be done in a specific part of the athlete's body, thus preventing many of the kinds of side effects seen with pharmaceuticals.

The deleterious side effects of steroids are well known. What if, instead of having to deal with pharmacological side effects, a gene could be introduced solely into particular muscle groups, resulting in localized, controlled muscle development?

Baseball players will likely first try using gene therapy for the familiar target of strength enhancement. Several researchers are investigating whether gene therapy can combat muscular degenerative diseases by enhancing muscle growth. The labs of Dr. H. L. Sweeney and collaborators have shown that introducing the gene IGF into rats results in greater muscle gain after exercise when compared to untreated rats. Targeted injections of viruses carrying IGF into specific muscle groups could produce rapid gains in strength. Genes may be identified that increase the proportion of fast-twitch fibers within muscles. Having a greater percentage of fast-twitch fibers in a ballplayer's muscles could enhance his explosiveness and speed.

A little imagination suggests many other potential illicit uses for gene therapy. As the differences in genes among individuals are better mapped out and understood, it may become clear that some gene variant combinations lead to better overall athletic performance. Parents with sufficient means might wish to introduce these favorable genes into their children. There are already cases of "manufactured athletes," such as the infamous case of quarterback Todd Marinovich and many of today's top tennis stars.

While complex traits like hand-eye coordination and other motor skills are likely controlled by far too many genes to be easily engineered, other structural qualities like ligament and cartilage strength, superior eyesight, or rapid muscle recovery may be susceptible to changes in just one or two genes. Already medical researchers are experimenting with ways of speeding bone, cartilage, and ligament healing with gene therapy agents. Pitchers might decide to preempt the threat of ligament damage by using gene therapy to periodically strengthen their elbow ligaments.

THE DARK SIDE OF THE GENE

The perceived attractions of technologies like gene therapy are threefold: strong, targeted results; difficult detection; and presumably fewer detrimental side effects. But is that last really true? In theory, the ability to introduce a specific gene or genes into a given muscle group or tissue should provide targeted and local effects that won't bleed over and manifest themselves in the rest of the body. Gene therapy, however, does carry its own risks. They can be divided into the categories neatly summarized by Secretary of Defense Donald Rumsfeld as the "known unknowns . . . and the unknown unknowns."

First, the known unknowns: insertion sites. When genes are introduced via gene therapy, the carrier of choice is a virus. If an athlete is after stable, long-term expression of the introduced gene, he or she will want to use a retroviral vector that will permanently insert DNA into that athlete's cells. Insertions occur at random locations within the DNA of the cell the virus entered. The DNA in the cell can be thought of as a huge stretch of countryside; the gene being introduced is a parachutist who has no idea of how to control his landing. If the parachutist lands in a field, that's great, but there may be problems if he veers into the trees. Similarly, a gene could land anywhere in the cell's copy of the genome, and this could lead to undesirable effects.

In one possible scenario, the introduced gene may land so close to another gene that it becomes affected by that neighboring gene's own controls. Often in gene therapy, the gene being introduced is designed to be turned on at a specific level in order to produce a specific effect. The consequences of landing near another gene might confound the intended results. Let's say the introduced gene lands near another gene that is turned on at a very high level. The introduced gene may also become turned on at a high level—higher than the gene doper would want. This could lead to unwanted results, especially if the introduced gene codes for a hormone or other product that is meant to be present in low quantities.

If an athlete, for example, wanted to increase his or her endogenous production of erythropoietin (EPO) in order to increase oxygen-carrying capacity, an insertion in the wrong place could lead to excessive EPO and a rapid increase in the number of red blood cells in the blood, beyond healthy levels. Blood with too many red cells becomes thick, leading to greater strain on the heart and a greater risk of blood clots, strokes, and heart attacks.

Another problem can occur if an introduced gene inserts near or within a gene, and changes the expression of that gene in ways that lead to health problems. In a well-publicized experiment in 2003, two of fourteen children participating in a gene therapy trial to correct their X-linked severe combined immunodeficiency (X-SCID) came down with T-cell leukemia as a direct result of their treatment. The gene therapy had been successful in treating their damaged immune systems, but the location at which the introduced gene inserted led to a completely different disease.

The other potential drawbacks to gene therapy are the "unknown unknowns." Much of what has been described in this chapter relies on the assumption that in the future we will know and understand much more about what kinds of genetic variants exist in the human population, what effect they have on traits like athletic performance, and how different gene variants work together. But we won't know everything. Introduced genes may act in unpredictable and harmful ways. While this seems unlikely given what we currently know about how the genes and proteins in a cell interact, the possibility exists. Unfortunately, given that the severe side effects of current performance-enhancing drugs like steroids are well known but don't dissuade athletes from using those drugs, the threat of the unknown is unlikely to keep athletes from trying the genetic option.

FINDING THE NEEDLE IN THE GENETIC HAYSTACK

How will baseball and other professional bodies act to detect and deter the abuse of these new genetic technologies for performance enhancement? Already sports governing bodies are looking ahead. The World Anti-Doping Agency has funded several research projects aimed at using genomic technologies to detect evidence of gene doping and has sponsored a workshop on the potential abuse of gene therapy in sports. Frédéric Donzé of WADA calls gene doping "likely to happen. As the technology of gene therapy advances, there will be those with means and motivation who will be willing to try."

One of the problems in detecting gene doping is that genes might be inserted only into particular muscles or tissues, and might produce proteins that are virtually identical to the proteins already produced by the user's body. Right now the most reliable way to detect gene doping is to take a biopsy sample of the tissue in question and see whether any evidence of gene doping—such as DNA from specific viruses—is present. Issues of civil liberties aside, simple aversion to pain means that very few athletes will willingly agree to a large-bore needle being stuck into their major muscle groups several times a year for sampling purposes. Several tools made possible by genomic research may offer the best hope for catching gene dopers. One of these, an assay called a microarray, can measure those genes in the body that are turned on and off at a given time, and to what degree. It provides a "fingerprint" of what's going on in the body's cells. When a performance-enhancing substance is introduced and used at a high dosage, there are telltale signs of which genes are being turned on and off.

If, for example, a microarray test of an athlete's blood shows that many of the genes turned on by human growth hormone are highly elevated in that sample, that would provide circumstantial evidence that the athlete had taken HGH. With gene doping, other gene-expression fingerprints could be screened to see if unexpected and incriminating genes were being turned on or off.

Once scientists learn more about genetic variation among people and how the many different variants work, another tool that may become useful is rapid genotyping. Genotyping involves analyzing a person's DNA to identify the hundreds of thousands of tiny differences that make that person unique. From this list of gene variants, or genotype, it may be possible to predict how high we'd expect that athlete's key genes to be turned on, setting a genetic baseline. If a gene such as IGF were turned on at a much higher level than expected, this would again be evidence that something beyond normal athletic conditioning is going on.

Other technologies, such as mass spectrometry, which can identify proteins within a biological sample, may one day become sensitive enough to detect the presence of anomalous proteins. Mass spectrometry can also be used to identify small molecules like hormones and custom-designed drugs. As anti-doping agencies increase their lists of the chemicals, hormones, and proteins that could lead to performance enhancement, mass spectrometry may be able to catch up to the chemical synthesis labs and ensure that an athlete is not artificially producing a performance-enhancing substance via gene doping.

Drug testing and prevention may also need to rely on the threat of future technological advancements. There may be no immediate way to detect some of the kinds of performance-enhancing technologies on the horizon, but samples could be collected, frozen, and tested at later dates as more sophisticated methods of analysis are developed. This kind of threat probably won't mean much to most athletes, for whom glory and success in the present far outweigh any possibility of future shame and exposure.

Even if the means to detect gene doping, pharmacogenomics, and other future performance-enhancing technologies are developed, it is hard to predict how and if baseball will use them. Even should these new technologies enter baseball, it is unlikely that we'll see the development of a gene gap between the "naturals" and the "transgenics." Genes are not destiny. Environment plays a key role in how genes are turned on and off and how they contribute to the final organism.

There is still an incredible amount we don't know about how the feedback between genes and environment works. Baseball is about more than simple physical ability. No scientist has isolated a gene for pitching smarts or emotional drive or knowing how to track a flyball slicing into the gap.

At least, not yet.

12

Profile: The Creator

AT A POINT in my negotiations, I began wondering if I would ever actually meet him. He used an anonymous email system worthy of the CIA. To talk he would use nothing but pay phones and pre-paid, disposable cellular phones. Even then, the conversations were brief. He had better security than the witness-protection program. I have no idea what his real name is or where he lives—and honestly, I'm glad.

On the internet, anyone can be found. It struck me as a bit odd, perhaps ingenuous, that while most baseball fans could name BALCO's Victor Conte, no one, not even prosecutors, seemed to have any clue about the actual creator of THG. It took two weeks of phone calls, emails, and running in what often seemed to be concentric circles before I got an email from the man I came to know as "Dr. X."

To: Will Carroll
From: anon@anon.com
You have been asking the right questions to the right people. How can I contact you? X.

That simple email led to an eventual face-to-face meeting. Dr. X purports to be the original creator of THG, a claim I believe but cannot independently verify. Attempts to confirm this met obvious roadblocks, so I want to be clear that Dr. X *may* be perpetrating one of the most elaborate scams I've ever seen. If so, he's convinced me.

Our meeting took place in a mid-sized Midwestern airport. I left my Indianapolis home early, not knowing what complications would arise. Dr. X had left highly specific instructions about what I was supposed to do that day, leaving little doubt that if anything went off-key, or if he just didn't feel like it, I would drive home without a meeting and communication with him might end. It was the third time I'd been ready to meet him, only to get last-minute cancellations twice before.

In the few hours it took me to drive to our prescribed meeting place, I went over the notes I'd made from our instant-messaging conversation. I was to wear jeans, a white T-shirt, and an "appropriate" jacket. I was to have nothing in my pocket except one credit card and one bill no larger than a ten, plus my car key. There would be no recording devices, no notepad, and no cameras. I'd go to the location he gave me and take everything out of my pockets and put it in my hand. I'd described myself to him, and he made pains to be sure that I did not wear a hat and that he knew exactly which model of Oakley glasses I wore. It seemed to bother him that I wore an unusual style.

It took a bit of smooth talking to get a pass beyond security without a ticket. It was genius that he suggested we meet in an airport. My easy deception of Homeland Security aside, there are few more controlled, public, and safe places in America.

I was thirsty, unsure if buying a bottle of water would be against the rules. My rebellious nature (and being in place ten minutes before the agreed-upon time) led me to have that drink. I walked over to the place Dr. X had indicated and sat facing the aisle.

It wasn't ten minutes before a man in a wheelchair sat directly opposite me. The older skycap who pushed him there thanked him for the tip, but it was his heavy breathing I noticed. The man in the chair wasn't feeble; he was solid. The wheelchair, I was sure, held Dr. X. He looked across and pointed to the floor. Our agreed "password" was a sign-countersign that I'd posted to my web log just before leaving, a quote from Koko the Gorilla. I would say "Darn floor," a phrase that could be explained away if I happened to say it to the wrong person. He would reply with "Big bite," something that wouldn't be returned accidentally.

His motion to the floor was an invitation, I thought, so I moved across, sat down, and waited. I'm no espionage agent and wasn't sure how this was actually supposed to work. I crossed my leg to retie my shoe and said "Darn floor," as if I'd found gum on my Steve Maddens.

He popped a piece of candy into his mouth. "Big bite." This was it.

"Thank you for meeting with me," I said. The wheelchair was a nice touch. In the time I spent with him, I couldn't make an educated guess about his height. His hair was under a hat, and his eyes were too green to be anything but contacts. I'm relatively sure that he had some padding underneath his shirt. If asked, my description of him would only be accurate for "male."

"You've got thirty minutes before I'm back on a plane."

I popped the cork on the conversation, going right to the heart of what I hoped to talk about with him. "When did you create THG?"

He looked left and right, checking to see if anyone heard or at least reacted. "I wasn't the first, really. Do you know much about the structure? How much of this do I have to explain?"

"I understand the basics, but I'm no chemist."

He began talking and made a gesture as if he were writing. "It's not hard to make. A bunch of gear [the term many use for

[161]

anabolic steroids] out there is just home-brewed crap that is cheap and worth every penny. They buy stuff from China or the worst stuff someone brings back from Mexico. They spend a day on the web reading the boards and the websites that teach stoichometry and redox. Poof, they're an underground lab.

"It's cheap stuff, poor quality, and probably doesn't do much of anything. It's the pathetic losers looking not to have sand kicked in their faces, not real athletes, but it's where they start. The real athletes, the world-class ones that use my stuff, they can afford the good gear.

"At that level you'll get some Fina, maybe some Test or Winny," he said, referring to three commonly used steroids. Fina or Finaplix is a veterinary-only version of Trenbolone. Test is testosterone. Winny is Winstrol, usually the injectable form. "If they get any gains, it's usually not from the low-potency stuff they're cooking up in Mom's Crock-Pot or buying off the internet. I check out some of the boards, mostly for laughs. You see them posting pictures and bragging about themselves.

"Maybe it looks good to some fatbody who can't get a girl to talk to him without paying by the minute, but as far as results, man, it's the difference between night and day."

"What's the biggest difference between something you can make and something available in Mexico?" I asked.

"Well, it depends," he said, again gesturing. His arms were larger than average, if far from bodybuilder size, and the veins in his forearms were visible. His eyebrows looked a bit thickened underneath his hat. "There's good and bad down there. I haven't spent any real time worrying because I didn't want to smuggle something over the border. There's pretty much everything down there as far as the prescribables. Deca, Winny, Androgel—if you know where to ask, you don't usually need a prescription.

"Here's where it gets complicated and simple all at once. Finding gear, making gear—it isn't hard. If you want to get big, fine. Easy enough. Now you have to think about getting caught. That's where the money is."

I realized that he'd spent five minutes not answering my original question. "But when did you first make it?"

"No B.S. huh? Fine. I wasn't the first to make it. Someone else mixed the two and was passing it around to some bodybuilders when I heard about it. I think you know who I'm talking about. I'd been doing some masking gear for one of them, and he brought me some. I took it to a friend who has access to a chromatograph, and I noticed some things that I thought were pretty apparent.

"By mixing the two sets [steroids—THG is a combination of Gestrinone and Trenbolone] they'd gotten something I hadn't seen before. First, it wasn't about bulk, and second, it broke down differently than anything I'd seen before.

"It took me about two weeks to figure out that it was the fertility stuff [Gestrinone is normally used for infertility] as the base. That put me at a real disadvantage because you can't just order that. I had to find someone willing to get me some and make sure it was okay. I had a lot of friends in pharmacies, and they finally were able to find me a good source.

"By the time I started making it for sale, we had a whole racket down sending girls into these clinics to this doctor who'd write the pass [prescription] and we'd pay cash. Doctors love that, man. So we'd spend a couple hundred bucks, spin it a bit, and sell it for a couple thousand a lot. That's good business and easier than buying the raw hormonals from China, which you have to do eventually."

I was willing to let it go at some point, but not yet. "Again, when?"

"Oh, I guess I didn't say, did I? Late '98. We'd gotten it pretty close to what we ended up with early and just played with it a bit from there. It was the breakdown that really got it noticed."

[163]

It was this breakdown that made THG such a potent steroid and so difficult to catch. "Why does that breakdown make it so different?" I asked him.

"It's the perfect defense," he said, laughing slightly, catching himself and looking around. "I mean, they all break down. Deca takes forever, so only the idiots take it."

"And Jason Giambi," I mentioned.

"Exactly. That's just one of the problems with all this. I know I can trust me. That's about it. I'm talking to you because our friend—well, you know the story. The minute I give it to a distributor, I'm at risk. I can do every Miami Vice trick, and any reasonably intelligent person is going to have enough information to give to the Feds so that it will get back to me.

"The distributors have it even rougher. They give the stuff to athletes! The user can't be trusted at all, even though he has his name to lose in all this. You don't *ever* trust a user because—guess what? They're users. They'll lie, cheat, steal, kill their grandma to get what they want."

He was avoiding some of the questions he didn't enjoy. "I still don't quite understand the breakdown," I said, hoping to bring him back.

"Yeah, yeah, everything breaks down. Deca takes about twelve months in a normal person, with some plus/minus. There's a trade-off between the effective period and the detectable period. Orals aren't detectable for nearly as long as shooters, but they have to take more or bigger doses. There's also the advantage of being oral, I guess.

"Where my stuff was better than anything else was that the test itself broke it down. You put it through the wringer and ninety-nine times out of a hundred, even if it was there, the tests would essentially clean themselves."

"How did they finally catch it, then?" I asked.

"You know the story. Some pissed-off coach was sick of hearing Conte brag about his athletes. That's what brought him down—he was rubbing people's face in it. There's some invisible line of winning or breaking records, or whatever his goal was for all this, and just standing up there on the medal stand giving the other people the finger."

The story, for those who don't know, is that Trevor Graham is the coach who sent the THG sample to the U.S. Anti-Doping Agency. Graham, the coach of 2004 Olympic hundred-meter champion Justin Gatlin and two-hundred-meter champion Shawn Crawford, admitted to being the whistleblower just weeks after his athlete won the gold medal. Graham is also the former coach of Marion Jones and Tim Montgomery, two athletes accused of using illegal substances obtained from BALCO. According to grand jury testimony leaked to the *San Francisco Chronicle*, Graham himself provided PEDs to his athletes. Gatlin had been suspended for his use of an attention-deficit disorder drug earlier in his career.

"That coach got hold of Conte's gear and sent it down to Catlin [Don Catlin, head of the UCLA Drug Testing Lab]. That SOB put it in a syringe. Come on—why hasn't anybody made a big deal about that? I mean, that's the most ridiculous thing so far. A syringe for an oral? The whole idea is to avoid syringes! I've seen those syringes that look like pens or markers or other things, but this didn't need it at all." He shook his head at what he saw as something incredible. "Everybody knows he [Graham] was juicing his guys too. Forget do the right thing; Graham was just keeping his advantage. Take out Conte and [Graham's] got the best stuff on the block, and you know where that comes from." There are, I discovered, at least five other distributors.

We paused a moment as a group of travelers passed by, and decided to move a couple of rows back to avoid more people. When we began to talk again, I dug back in on the testing. "So, not only did they not know what they were looking for with your 'gear,' the test itself was destructive to the process. It was a bonus, and that's the reason it was so successful."

"Yes," he said, seeming proud. "It was part of the compound. To do the normal tests like mass spectrometry, the sample ends up drying out. My stuff breaks down when it's dry. It made it a bit of a problem for people trying to store it—it has to be kept in suspension [liquid form]—but that was fine with me. They wouldn't buy more than they could sell, and there would be the inevitable spoilage, meaning they'd end up coming back for more."

"Let me make this clear," I said. "You never had any contact with athletes, never sold them your stuff?"

"Not zero contact. I'd go to shows like Columbus [the Arnold Classic, the major bodybuilding competition and trade show held yearly in Columbus, Ohio] and such, so I'd see guys, and I know a few of them knew who I was. I've written some articles. I don't need the athletes like the distributors do. For them, it's customer and advertising all in one. You saw Conte there acting like a rock star, putting him and Bonds in ads for his zinc. Give me a break."

"Didn't you wonder which athletes were using your stuff?"

"No," he said matter-of-factly. "I don't need the justification. I don't have that kind of ego. I know my stuff is the best gear out there. I hear who's working with who, so I have an idea. I know who's winning."

I wanted to know more about the creation and chemistry. "How did you test this? You said you had it quickly, then made adjustments. Couldn't some of these 'adjustments' be toxic?"

He just shook his head, indicating he wasn't going to answer. He took a deep breath and said, "Sometimes cats."

I wasn't quite ready to let it go. "Liver toxicity is just one of the problems, or has that been removed from your stuff?"

He thought about this answer before responding. "Not removed. The best stuff is actually related to a really toxic compound.

I'm not going to try and explain the differences to you because short of a degree in chemistry, which I know you don't have . . ."

"I got a B in O-Chem," I said. His look dismissed me.

"I don't want to play toxicity down, especially hepatotoxicity. I can do the chemistry, and we can find out which ones work and which ones don't. Something that drops someone is worse than one that just doesn't work. If I make ten runs of gear, one will work. Four won't do anything, or not the right things, and five will be toxic."

This number surprised me. "Half? Half will be toxic?"

"Different levels of toxic. I'm not talking about rat poison, but risky. 19-nor is real close to my stuff, but that won't break down at all. It's maybe the best gear I've ever seen, better than Test even, and that's the gold standard. Downside is that it's just poison in the liver. I've seen guys that took a Halo stack [a combination of Halotestin, a potent steroid, and another steroid in hopes that the combination will raise the efficacy of both drugs] in megadoses that didn't have the problems people have on a low-dose of 19-nor gear."

I wasn't familiar with what he was referring to as "19-nor." Later I discovered that in 1966 researchers in Germany had developed a steroid known as methyltrienelone. It was very similar, chemically, to an oral Trenbolone, one of the bases for THG. Methyltrienelone had what has been described as both exceptional androgenic properties and exceptional liver toxicity. The drug was never approved for use in any form but is made for scientific research purposes. That availability, even in a controlled manner, makes it something of a holy grail for many users.

There is very little research available on whether methyltrienelone is as effective as some say. Experts in the field have been quoted as saying it is the "perfect anabolic." Those who use the drug seldom survive long enough to record any effect. If nothing else, it may indeed be the perfect anabolic metaphor: superpowerful and deadly.

"So you have this gear that has most of the effectiveness, few of the side effects, and doesn't show up in tests," I said. "I can see why that might sell." If Dr. X were a pharmaceutical company—which in many ways he was—he would have a blockbuster on his hands. "And it's oral. That's something a lot of people forget. If there's an injectable and an oral of equal effectiveness, or even if the injectable is a bit more potent, most people are going to take the oral. Guys who do their homework and aren't buying their gear out of someone's basement know that oral breaks down quicker too. Say it this way: if someone's got to use a needle, they aren't trying hard enough."

Dr. X was "famous" because his drugs were undetectable for much of their existence. I wondered if he considered testing at all. "How much of a problem is testing?"

"What do you mean?" he asked, jabbing with his finger. "My gear doesn't show up. Is it a problem for the idiots using Deca or Androgel and praying they don't get tested? Yeah, but life is a problem for them. That's why I don't deal with the athletes much. I don't like having to explain everything to them. Most of these guys aren't much more than savants with a physical skill or two. Most of the stuff I'm saying to you, I think you get. To them, even if they hear me, all they care about is what it gets them."

"Does that make dosing a problem?" I asked.

"Sure. When I look at the gear we give out, we're looking at things like effective period, the catabolization and metabolization, the hepatotoxicity, the effects, everything. The athlete is looking at how big, how fast. Period.

"They don't care about anything until it happens. Someone tells them they're not strong enough, not fast enough, they won't believe it. Their entire identity is wrapped up in being number one. Someone passes them, what are they then? Some can rationalize it, I guess, and say their time is up. Others can't, and they start looking for a new edge. [Tim] Montgomery was like that, I hear. Just had to find the next new things, wouldn't let anyone get ahead of him.

"That's how he ended up with [Marion] Jones. She was number one. I think they have a kid. Getting close to number one had to rub off on him. Of course, there was a lot of chemical rubbing too. It's why I won't have anything to do with the athletes. All my time is spent educating people about the effects, positive and negative, and then the rest is in the lab, working on what's next."

What's next was very important. "You said that THG was first made several years back and that Conte's been using it for at least four years. Where does that put it?"

"THG is three generations back. If it hadn't been blown up with the test, I don't think very many people would be using it now. I know there's at least one other formulation of THG out there, and bodybuilders might use it. People are using Deca still, and we know the problems with that. The knowledge is ten generations back or more.

"Look at Deca. You told me Giambi admitted he used Deca?" I nodded, and he just shook his head. "You take Deca, there's a whole series of things that you have to take to make it worthwhile, unless you're just an absolute freaking chump. I'm going to give him the benefit of the doubt. He ended up at BALCO, and he'd been around people who knew what they were doing. . . ."

"What do you mean by that?" I asked. He just shook his head. I sighed, wondering where that line might have gone and said, "Go ahead."

"So here is this guy with all the money in the world who's taking something you can find at Gold's Gym? Was he stacking it? Was he taking anti-estrogens to keep him from growing tits? I'd want to know if he was taking something to keep his wife from figuring it out. Is he married?"

I couldn't remember all the details, but I knew that Giambi was married now. Since he allegedly was using as early as 1999, it's something that would be interesting to know, but unlikely that we ever will.

He continued. "I don't think Giambi or any guy would walk up there with a bat made in 1970, do you? He wouldn't wear some cleats from ten years ago, would he? So why is this guy—any guy who can afford better—taking something like this? You take Deca today, I can come back in 2006 and you're gonna pop [test positive]. In any kind of organization that tests, you can't use Deca and hope to come up clean.

"You can take THG, at least before 2004, and be guaranteed to come up clean. One of the guys on my stuff could walk into the test with a needle sticking out of his ass and not worry."

"I thought your stuff was oral," I asked. I was on the lookout for anything resembling an inconsistency in his story.

"THG is oral. It's light, and you can put it into anything except Coke and Kool-Aid."

"Why not those?"

"They're too acidic. I won't drink the stuff. You can clean pipes with them and it will just eat the rust right off. I've never done the research, but none of my gear is that dangerous."

"That's a big claim. I'd like to see that tested."

"So do it. The government is the one passing law after law that keeps us from doing it. Andro's illegal now, and no one can explain to me why. 1-Test is illegal, I think, but I can't get a straight answer. You want to know the effects of this type of thing, do a scientific test. Give me the ability to patent my gear and give me the same type of protections and tax breaks that the drug companies get and we'll know in a hurry what gear does."

I wanted to get back to the issue of his apparently inconsistent statement. "Back to what you said a minute ago—you said that THG was oral and left the sentence kind of hanging. Is the newer stuff not oral?"

He paused for a moment. I thought he was going to shake his head again, my question threatening the secrecy surrounding the steroids he'd developed that were likely to be in use today. "If you go back to the original stuff—what you know as THG or 'clear'— there's been three new developments since then.

"The first really didn't change anything, it just made it cheaper and easier to manufacture. The structure stayed the same, and we think that the same tests that Catlin developed after it got outed would detect this too.

"The second was a completely different structure, based on the original technique. The stuff was Gestrinone altered to act like another set of gear. This second stuff was another base altered to act like another set of gear. It isn't as good as the stuff, and it's a bit harder to produce. It got used, I know, pretty widely, and a couple of labs were able to fake it up pretty good. It's easy to reverse-engineer these things if you know what you're looking at.

"The third set of stuff has nothing to do with either of the first two. It's a whole new process that's more breakdown than buildup. I took out the element that creates the estrogen."

I was astounded. "It's the drug without the side effect?"

"It's not a drug," he said matter-of-factly.

"It's gear without the side effect?"

He smiled. "Yes."

"Undetectable?"

"So far."

It took me a moment to get my head around that. If what he was telling me was true, that the stuff Victor Conte said in his *ESPN The Magazine* article was available, then there was a "perfect anabolic" on the streets.

I was running out of time. A quick glance at my watch told me I only had about five minutes left and hours of questions I wanted to get to. "How do you deal with testing?"

"I don't. That's not my problem. Once it's out of my lab, it's not my problem."

I'd asked the question incorrectly. "I mean, when you're building your stuff, do you consciously consider whether or not it deals with testing? It sounds like with the original stuff, the breakdown under testing was more of a lucky break than a design feature."

"Yeah, that's accurate. Knowing that now, I can build around that. But no, it doesn't really matter to me what the testers do. I just have to be different enough. Let's say you take Deca and add an alkylate group to it. That's easy. High school chemistry."

"I didn't take that class."

"Okay, call it honors chemistry then. You can do that with anything—just tack on something as long as the equations work out and you don't get something that's toxic. You add on too much and you get side effects and such; add on too little and it shows up on tests. There's a smart happy medium where I can make something that can even enhance the base."

I needed clarification. "I understand this, I think. The metaphor I always hear is that when they run a test, it's like looking through a book of mug shots. If the mug shot isn't there, then it can't be identified."

"Exactly!" he said, showing the most excitement he had in our time together. "It's not just that they have to have the chemical signature, it's that they have to run that particular test. If the NFL wants to test for every known steroid, that's more than one hundred tests per player. Maybe an organization like that, with a very limited population and with that kind of money, they could do it. Thirty teams, fifty players, a hundred tests—that's a lot of tests, and they aren't cheap."

"And you're saying that even those will be ineffective."

"What's ineffective?" he asked me. "Are you trying to eliminate everything? Catch everyone that's using? Then you're going to fail or go broke. It costs me thirty or forty grand to develop one, and it costs double that to test one baseball team for every known substance. That's for every known substance—and I know for a fact there's ten out there they don't know about."

"How many labs are there like yours?"

"None!" he said, jabbing again. "No one else puts the same effort, has my experience, has the tools I have available to me. I can make my gear on equipment that most of the underground labs can only dream about. I've got guys working on projects that do pharm work the rest of the day.

"Even so, there are other labs that can do similar work. They have gear out there that's been used, that's good stuff. When there's as much money as there is, people will swarm to it. There's no money on the testing side. What's Catlin make? What's Black or Ayotte or any of those making? I make that in a month.

"And then there's the basement geniuses. There's thousands of guys cooking something in their mom's house thinking they've got the next Winny-V. Every once in a while, one of them is good or lucky. Most of them are just trying to make some good stuff for themselves. It's not stupid. You mix your own, you know what you're getting."

Before I was able to ask my next question, he turned his head—the next flight boarding was his. "Last question. I have to get pre-boarded because of this," gesturing to the wheelchair.

"What's your problem with all of this? I'm not going to ask you if you sleep at night, but I want to know if it worries you that kids are taking this stuff or if you see some of the more famous cases like Steve Courson or some of the bodybuilders and wrestlers."

He cut me off. "Prove that those cases come back to what they were taking and I'd worry more. Those guys had problems, and it had nothing to do with what they were taking. A lot of them were addicts. They didn't care what they were taking.

"You want to fix this? You want to make sure kids don't take this where it puts them in a bad situation? Legalize it. Let me do my work in the open, and give me the same advantages and disadvantages that all the other pharms do. Make my stuff prescription only, and make sure doctors monitor everyone that takes it. The toxic, amateur crap will still be out there, but no one will have any incentive to take it.

"And don't give me any sob story about it ruining sports. Football, baseball, hockey—no one says it isn't in those games already, and none of them are going broke. Maybe hockey, but that has nothing to do with this. More home runs mean more money. Bigger, faster linemen mean that Peyton Manning breaks every record in the books—unless one of those bigger, faster lineman breaks him in half.

"The pharm companies are already making money off this. There's drugs like Provigil, Casodex, and Androgel all on the streets, and I wonder why no one is watching to see why doctors are writing so many prescriptions for narcolepsy or prostate cancer for perfectly healthy young athletes. Show me the real will to handle the real problems and I'll be the biggest supporter. I'm sick of sitting here, looking over my shoulder.

"For me, this is about money. I'll make more money on the open market than I will like this."

As the call came for Dr. X's boarding, I thanked him for his time and asked if I could do some follow-ups. He just shook his head. Emails through the anonymous, secure system he used have not been returned since we met. Our conversation wasn't tape-recorded—he simply wouldn't allow it—but I quickly made notes after leaving. I believe this re-creation of our conversation to be extremely accurate. Again, I want to note that I have no hard evidence that this man is who he says he is—one of the creators of designer steroids, including the infamous THG—but I believe strongly that he is telling the truth. Frankly, it chills me to the core.

One last thing. As he left me, rolling back to the gate, he asked if I'd been a good player myself. I laughed and responded that anything he could give me wouldn't have helped.

"You look like an ex-player. Take some pounds off you and you'd be right back in it, wouldn't you?"

I'll admit it, I had to know. "You have something for that?"

"Give me six weeks and I'd have you in the best shape of your life." He winked at me, and for the first time I knew exactly what the term "Faustian" meant. I started to say something, but it was better to walk away, back to my car, and as far away as possible. More than once, I looked in the mirror.

13

Those in Favor Raise Their Hands

FOR A BALANCED LOOK at any issue, there has to be a willing-ness to look at all sides of it. In a matter as emotional as the use of performance-enhancing drugs, there are not only two sides but many; and there are no easy answers of good and bad. It's not the Wild West. People don't easily identify themselves with white or black Stetsons.

Some observers find it difficult to understand the motivations of athletes who use steroids and other performance-enhancing drugs. It's an even bigger step to try to understand those who advocate or defend that usage. But it's an important step to take. You'll find a credible case when you speak to the right people. But finding these credible voices is difficult: they are often drowned out by a subculture that is beyond understanding.

In forums that discuss how to use drugs like MıT, a new steroid with toxicity approaching that of freebasing Drano, intelligent voices are seeking to turn the supplement industry into a self-policing group that truly seeks the highest ideals of quality of product and quality of life. Some people believe that the products they use, even when illegal, need to be used properly and are willing to stick their necks out to get the information to the users. There are evangelists, true believers, and muscle-heads. There are doctors, lawyers, and chemists.

It's an interesting, often disturbing journey to find these people. In planning for this book, I'd actually tracked down a local steroid dealer, thinking this was the real face of the steroid advocate. But I discovered that equating the "pro-steroid" advocate with a simple drug pusher is not only oversimplistic, it's simply wrong.

My research brought me to a pair of men, one an educated white-collar professional who has become a leading voice in the steroid community, the other a man who says he "builds beasts." One is a lawyer with credentials that would take up the better part of a page, the other is a man who relies on experience and results. What they have in common is a substantive point of view that I find compelling.

My first conversation was with Rick Collins, a respected attorney and one of a few who specialize in steroid and steroid-related cases. He is also a consultant for several supplement companies. His firm of Collins, McDonald, and Gann is legal adviser to the International Federation of Bodybuilders, the Weider-founded organization that is to bodybuilders what MLB is to baseball. He is also the author of *Legal Muscle: Anabolics in America*, considered by many to be the definitive text on steroid law.

I began by trying to find out what led Collins to focus on this area of law, an admittedly small niche. "I attended Hofstra University, here in New York, for both undergrad and law," he told me. "I had discovered bodybuilding in my teens, and by college I was competing and winning trophies in local bodybuilding contests. My college grades were very good, and I was fortunate to be offered a full academic scholarship to law school. That wasn't a deal I could afford to pass up.

"I served on the Law Review in school and then went to work as a prosecutor, fighting violent crimes and serious, non-steroid, drug cases. From all my time in gyms, I knew people, and when a few of them got 'busted' for crimes involving steroids, they called me. Over the years, one case led to another.

"Now the criminal-defense portion of my practice almost exclusively involves bodybuilding drug offenses. I also do legal work for many dietary supplement companies. I think I can very safely say that I've been involved in more steroid-related legal matters than any other lawyer. I love what I do. How often do criminal defense lawyers genuinely like, respect, and really connect with most of their clients? Arguably, there's only so much you should have in common with rapists, robbers, crackheads, and the like."

Of course, anyone remotely connected to steroids, even as an attorney, seems to be himself suspect of steroid use. Collins is certainly in great shape, so I asked him how he was introduced to the world of steroids. "I never answer personal questions like that out of respect to the privacy of people I care about. I'll leave tattle-telling to Jose Canseco." This wasn't going to be easy, I could tell.

I asked Collins how many legal cases involving steroids are filed in a given year. "Nobody knows. The number is small in federal courts, but the vast majority are brought in state and local courts where no reliable statistics exist to my knowledge." That's right, even the leading expert in this field can't find reliable statistics regarding this type of case. The disorganization in this area of law is surprising.

It seems that the most misused word in any discussion about performance-enhancing drugs is "legal." The word is used for situations involving sports sanctioning bodies and state and federal legislation. I asked Collins to define the term "legal" in the purely legal sense.

He immediately began to correct me. "The proper term for these drugs in the context of sports sanctioning bodies would be "banned" rather than "illegal." Their proscription in sports is founded on administrative rules, not actual laws. They are typically called banned substances.

"Outside of sports, laws apply to drugs such as anabolic steroids and growth hormone. To simply say 'steroids are illegal' is a gross oversimplification. Heroin is illegal because it has no valid medical purpose. So is marijuana. They are Schedule I controlled substances. Steroids are illegal to possess without a prescription for a valid medical purpose, but they are perfectly *legal* when possessed or used for a variety of valid medical reasons. The legality or illegality is based on the context. They are Schedule III drugs."

Collins also didn't like my use of the term "performance-enhancing drugs." "It's vague and arguably unhelpful. For example, caffeine is a performance-enhancing drug and in fact resulted in a violation under Olympic doping rules for many years when detected above a certain concentration. The term seeks to depict steroids within a specific context of use. It's not the only use."

While I still like the definition of PEDs and IPEDs, I was willing to go with Collins's more legal and proper definitions. I asked him how PEDs were treated differently from other controlled substances. "Some PEDs are not controlled substances at all, others are," he told me, still deriding my term. "Let's talk about anabolic steroids, most descriptively called anabolic-androgenic steroids, or AAS. AAS fall within Schedule III of the federal Controlled Substances Act—the same legal class as barbiturates, ketamine, LSD precursors, and narcotic painkillers such as Vicodin. AAS are the only hormones listed in the entire law.

"Testosterone, the 'king' of AAS but also a naturally occurring hormone present in the body of every human being, is a criminalized substance under the statute. Under federal law, personal-use possession of AAS is a misdemeanor, distribution is a felony—as with other controlled substances. Human growth hormone is not treated as a controlled substance in mere possession situations under federal law.

"But state laws vary widely. In some states, such as Rhode Island, both AAS and growth hormone are controlled substances. Pennsylvania, on the other hand, has gone out of its way to say that growth hormone 'shall not be included as an anabolic steroid.' Let's take the typical first-time possession of a small quantity of 'juice' for personal use. In Connecticut it's a misdemeanor, with at worst up to a year in jail unless it occurs near a school, in which case there's additional imprisonment. In Arizona it's technically a felony, but under a new law eligible offenders get probation with drug treatment in lieu of prison.

"In Colorado a bizarre distinction makes using a misdemeanor but possessing it a felony! In Florida and Georgia, simple possession of any amount is a felony with up to five years' imprisonment, and in Alabama it's a felony with up to ten years in prison! In Louisiana you can face imprisonment with hard labor for a first offense of mere personal-use possession!

"In my book I spell out and explain the law of every state. In practice, most first-time offenders with small quantities do not get prison time. Possession of larger amounts, or situations of manufacture, importation, or distribution, can more often result in jail or prison sentences."

Because he is a consultant and attorney to some of the best-known supplement companies in America, the recent controversies surrounding anabolic-type substances and prohormones is of special concern to Collins. I asked him about this new area of concern and how it has affected his practice. Collins knew the law cold, giving me a very technical breakdown. "On October 22, 2004, President Bush signed into law the Anabolic Steroid Control Act of 2004, scheduled to take effect ninety days later. Ratified by the U.S. Congress earlier in the month, the bill expanded the steroid law that had been passed in 1990. The new law also provides $15 million for educational programs for children about the dangers of anabolic steroids, and directs the U.S. Sentencing

Commission to consider revising federal guidelines to increase the penalties for steroid possession and distribution.

"The law, which took effect January 20, 2005, adds twenty-six new steroid compounds to the previous list of substances that are legally defined as 'anabolic steroids' and classified as Schedule III controlled substances. Mere possession of any of these products will be a basis for arrest and prosecution as a federal drug criminal." Collins provided a list of these newly controlled substances. It reads like a witches' brew: androstanediol, androstanedione, androstenediol, androstenedione, bolasterone, calusterone, 1-dihydrotestosterone (a.k.a. "1-testosterone"), furazabol, 13b-ethyl-17a-hydroxygon-4-en-3-one, 4-hydroxytestosterone, 4-hydroxy-19-nortestosterone, mestanolone, 17a-methyl-3b, 17b-dihydroxy-5a-androstane, 17a-methyl-3a,17b-dihydroxy-5a-androstane, 17a-methyl-3b, 17b-dihydroxyandrost-4-ene, 17a-methyl-4-hydroxynandrolone, methyldienolone, methyltrienolone, 17a-methyl-1-testosterone, norandrostenediol, norandrostenedione, norbolethone, norclostebol, normethandrolone, stenbolone, and tetrahydrogestrinone.

Some of these new substances have been widely marketed as dietary supplements, such as androstenedione, norandrostenedione, norandrostenediol, 1-testosterone, and 4-hydroxytestosterone. Others, such as bolasterone, calusterone, furazabol, and stenbolone, are actually very old pharmaceutical steroids that were missed in the original federal law. These dusty old compounds were likely included after the highly publicized reemergence of norbolethone (also added to the list) in an Olympic urine sample. Also listed is tetrahydrogestrinone, or THG, the so-called "designer steroid" that precipitated the BALCO scandal, but the list does not include DMT and another designer steroid that has not been released.

Afterward I was able to go to a local sports nutrition store and find bottles of several of these now-controlled substances still on the shelf. It wasn't an isolated incident; three separate stores had at least two newly controlled substances available for sale. Strangely, it wasn't ignorance of the law that seemed to be the problem. Clerks at all three stores were aware that new laws had gone into effect. "Sure, a lot of guys came in mid-January to stock up on stuff like 1-test and andro," one manager told me. It seemed the problem was that there were simply so many bottles with so many ingredients, some were simply overlooked. The clerks weren't terribly concerned about any consequences.

Collins continued, "The law also changes the general requisite elements of an anabolic steroid. The 'promotes muscle growth' language that precedes the list of 1990s compounds is now removed from the statute. Strangely, an anabolic steroid, under the new law, need not promote muscle growth. It simply needs to be chemically and pharmacologically related to testosterone, and either on the new list of substances or any salt, ester, or ether of a substance on the list. The omission of the criterion of promoting muscle growth profoundly eases the process by which a newly created designer steroidal compound may be scheduled.

"Even under the 1990 law, the attorney general had the authority to schedule additional or newly discovered steroidal compounds without going back to Congress for approval. But under the old law, in order for a compound to qualify as an anabolic steroid, the attorney general was required to prove that the compound had anabolic properties.

"Under the new law, this is no longer a requirement, making the process much simpler. Rather, the attorney general must only establish that the compound is chemically and pharmacologically related to testosterone. Litigation may be required to explore what 'pharmacologically related' means with respect to steroidal compounds." In other words, Collins's legal workload is only on the rise.

Some exceptions were built into the law, Collins told me. After a protracted battle on the issue in Congress, the law permits the continued sale of DHEA as a dietary supplement by adding it to the list of other hormonal substances (estrogens, progestins, and corticosteroids) excluded from the law. It is corticosteroids that are often injected into the joints of players, allowing them to continue playing despite pain and inflammations. Collins also pointed out that the law fixes some of the mistakes and poor draftsmanship of the 1990 law. But at least one typographical error in the new law was apparent during an initial review by independent chemists: "13b-ethyl-17a-hydroxygon-4-en-3-one" (a de-methylated version of norbolethone) should read "13b-ethyl-17b-hydroxygon-4-en-3-one." You can understand the error, I'm sure.

As complicated as this all sounds, it's actually worse. Due to the nature of the substances and the legal ramifications, there is no "gatekeeper" to discern if persons should use the substance or to educate them about proper usage. For most drugs in America, that gatekeeper is the physician. "Given that there are some valid medical uses, why aren't these simply prescription drugs rather than a controlled substance?" I asked.

"They used to be. The Anabolic Control Act of 1990 changed all that," Collins explained, "by making them into a controlled substance. While doctors can still prescribe them, it can't be for 'performance enhancement' or for cosmetic reasons. That didn't stop demand, of course, and so the black market has ballooned. Today most AAS on the black market are foreign veterinary preparations of questionable content. Personally I think the War on Drugs approach has failed.

"The overwhelming majority of the many hundreds of AAS users with whom I've consulted are not competitive athletes but rather cosmetic users simply seeking a better body. Their motivations are much more analogous to those who use diet pills or seek liposuction or breast augmentation."

Despite this, it's well known that some physicians, especially inside the sports world, are involved in helping athletes, whether through prescriptions or merely by obtaining the necessary physical tests to ensure health during the use of some of these substances. I asked Collins, "If physicians seek to help athletes using AAS, what legal risk, if any, do they take?"

Collins again demonstrated his knowledge, drawing up statutes off the top of his head. "Under federal law and regulations, physicians may lawfully prescribe a controlled substance, including AAS, only for legitimate medical reasons—which would not include enhancing sports performance in healthy athletes. Some states have even enacted specific legislation to make it a crime for doctors to prescribe AAS for bodybuilding. Physicians may face disciplinary action from their state medical licensing boards or in some cases criminal prosecution under state or federal laws."

It seemed to me that Collins thought the use of what he called AAS was more akin to elective cosmetic surgery than what we often think of as the use of illicit drugs. He agreed with that assessment. I noted that there were problems with the model. "I think you'd agree we don't want these substances in the hands of minors. Would changing how we use and monitor these drugs to your model better accomplish this?"

"Not only would I agree," he replied, "but I'll go further. They also shouldn't be in the hands of anyone using them to cheat others." This statement came as something of a surprise to me. Collins continued, "Cheating harms others, not just oneself. Sports sanctioning bodies have a right to impose rules to ensure fairness—the so-called level playing field. So if the rules of a sport forbid the use of a substance, and a player knowingly uses it, he's a cheater and deserving of punishment. And the 'everybody's doing it' excuse is moral relativism that just doesn't wash.

"Our present model removes physicians from the steroid equation, relegating all but very limited medical uses to a ballooning and unregulated black market of substandard foreign veterinary drugs which are used in the complete absence of medical supervision. Does that sound good? Prohibition works better in theory than in practice. The potential health risks of AAS usage have been increased, not diminished, by this approach.

"Ironically, you might say that the Anabolic Steroid Control Act has left us with little or no control over the distribution of anabolic steroids. Permitting knowledgeable doctors to enter the equation of aesthetic AAS administration—without fear of arrest and prosecution—to certain appropriate, mature adults would greatly diminish the black market. Shrinking the black market would push up prices, making it more difficult for teens to afford the drugs. Further, and important, penalties for those who knowingly sell AAS to minors could be increased, providing a stronger disincentive for anyone to do so. The result would protect teens, maintain fairness in sports, preserve civil liberties, and enhance public safety."

I continued, "When it comes to media treatment of PEDs, there's an 'everybody's doing it' mentality. Do you feel their use is as broad as the media would have us believe?"

"I don't think everybody in sports is doing it," Collins said. "But I do believe that contemporary drug-testing technology is quite imperfect, and that the number of those who get caught does not reflect the total number of those who are using, which is undoubtedly higher." Collins is no baseball expert, but he was able to address some of the recent claims that as many as 80 percent of major league baseball players are using AAS. Of course, survey testing conducted in 2003 showed just over 5 percent of players testing positive. While there were obviously some players who slipped through by using nonbanned substances (THG wasn't tested for at that time, nor banned) or other methods, I asked Collins for a realistic estimate based on his expert opinion.

"Not only are there nonbanned substances, there are also explicitly banned substances that are *not* tested for, such as human growth hormone," he said. HGH tests are still very controversial, but all agree that at the very least a blood test is necessary. "Any attempt at an estimate would be highly speculative. Obviously a single digit number is ridiculous, but 80 percent also strikes me as wildly inflated. The truth, as is so often the case, lies somewhere in between."

I pointed out to Collins that the first athlete who tests positive under baseball's new testing policy is going to have a hard time in the court of public opinion, certainly taking more scrutiny and scorn than the all-but-unknowns of track or bodybuilding might face. But would they have much basis for appealing their test?

"Appeals in drug-testing cases are always an option if there are irregularities in the collection process, chain of custody of the sample, or testing protocol," he explained patiently. "While most anti-doping programs approach a standard of 'strict liability,' some provide for leniency in cases of unknowing consumption." This, of course, is the line of defense of several of those who have testified in the BALCO case, including Barry Bonds.

One thing had really surprised me in Collins's book. It seemed that physicians and some drug-control agencies actually lobbied *against* the new laws. "The chapter on the criminalization of AAS in *Legal Muscle* is really eye-opening. It seems the stance toward AAS, by both government and sanctioning bodies, is more posturing than genuine concern for either the sport or the athletes. Why were the voices of drug enforcement and medicine not heard?"

Collins answered, "They were heard, but they were disregarded because the problem of steroid cheating in sports, and the permissive message it sends to young people, was seen as requiring a strong statement of condemnation by politicians. Unfortunately, cynics would say that this type of legislation is much better at giving the appearance of self-serving elective officials' concern over an issue than actually solving it. Prohibition-type legislation often has unintended consequences.

"Most people are shocked to learn that the DEA, FDA, and AMA all stood up *against* making AAS into controlled substances, but that Congress went ahead anyway," he continued. "Another interesting point is that the media almost always present AAS in the context of sports cheating. It would seem that steroid use is inherently unethical, regardless of legalities.

"Making more things into controlled substances won't banish them from Olympic and pro sports. That hasn't stopped the cheaters. The laws are already on the books, but how often do you see a sports celebrity arrested for steroids? It's mostly the guys in the local gyms who don't play any sports at all that are getting dragged out of their houses in handcuffs. They're not national, million-dollar role models for kids. They're just adults trying to look better at the beach."

While I doubt that the average guy trying to look better in a bathing suit reaches for a vial of Superdrol, Collins has a point. "Your clients, as you point out, are seldom million-dollar athletes, just regular guys and even gals. Who are your typical clients, what is the typical crime they are being charged with, and what is the typical penalty they face?" I asked.

"My typical AAS clients are twenty-five to forty-five years of age, gainfully employed, dedicated to working out, acutely concerned about their physical appearance, and nonsmokers. Ironically, they tend to be more health conscious than the average American, and probably are healthier, given the epidemic of obesity and associated diseases like diabetes, cardiovascular disease, and cancer.

"They are typically arrested because they are caught in possession of AAS without a prescription, often after ordering the AAS over the internet. Even those who receive no jail time can suffer a variety of significant consequences. For example, drug convictions can be a bar to holding certain professional and other licenses and to college financial aid, and can jeopardize present and future employment."

Collins had mentioned earlier that he felt most AAS comes from international veterinary sources. I told him of some of my research into the issue, which disagreed with that assessment. Collins gave a little ground, saying, "True there has been an explosion of 'underground labs' making some variant of AAS—or at least it appears to be an explosion. Obviously the internet has led what was once a discussion at the downtown gym to become a discussion on an AAS-focused website. While the number of domestic underground operations does appear to have grown, most AAS still come from Mexico, Asia, and Eastern Europe."

Collins had also thought through the next frontier. I asked, "How will changes in AAS technologies, such as genetics, affect the law?"

"So far, the development of these substances has stayed well ahead of detection methods and legislative efforts," he said. "The use of gene manipulation may render AAS largely obsolete. Steroids are simply one of today's tools to cheat in sports, but tomorrow is always a day away."

With all the legislation supplanting regulation, I asked Collins if he felt the supplement industry had done a good job regulating itself, or whether the willingness of athletes to pay top dollar for questionable quality was bringing too many scammers into that market due to lack of regulation.

Collins conceded, "There is definite room for improvement within the supplement industry, but contrary to some claims there already are regulatory controls in place if FDA will simply enforce them. Don't forget that from a general comparative risk standpoint, supplements are safer than drugs."

COLLINS HAD ALREADY been more than generous with his time and so I took my leave, with a load of information and perhaps some new ways to think about things. My next appointment, however, was more in line with what the typical, uninformed person would think of as a "black hat." Where Collins makes a clear delineation on certain issues, including the use of PEDs in sport, L Rea does not. Where Collins cuts a sharp if slightly imposing profile in a tailored pinstripe suit, L Rea is more likely to be seen in public with his shirt off and muscles bulging.

Rea, who is also regularly referred to as "Author L Rea," uses a pseudonym not to hide but to enhance. He frequents several of the top bodybuilding websites and discussion boards where he is acknowledged as one of the leading minds in the game. His unrepentant attitude toward substances differentiates him from many, perhaps due to his touting himself as a "biochemistry expert." To Rea, the human body is art, just waiting to be driven to its ultimate potential.

That potential, as has been demonstrated by Rea's protégé, the professional bodybuilder Toney Freeman, can be awe-inspiring. Freeman at six feet two inches is a 280-pound block of chiseled ebony. The Indiana native has biceps as big as some men's legs and a waist that, at thirty inches, is smaller than that of the average man on the street. His massive chest and back are almost superhuman. Freeman credits his body to hard work and the coaching of L Rea.

Rea has some controversial ideas, ones that he is often attacked for, especially by those who have the academic credentials that Rea admittedly lacks. "Test-tube studies and quoting other people's work lacks the personal knowledge required at this level," he said in a recent interview. "It seems unlikely that [doctors] would condone the criteria necessary to create testing procedures for the in-lab validation and peer review of my work." Rea is perfectly happy to show off his results, if not his research, every time he unleashes one of his beasts.

He is the author of two books, *Chemical Muscle Enhancement* and *Building the Perfect Beast*, and has plans for a third in the series called *Domination*. Rea isn't much for subtlety, as you can tell. He's also the author of hundreds of articles for muscle and bodybuilding magazines and websites.

For competitive athletes, Rea's time can cost in the thousands. I was happy he agreed to speak with me while withholding the bill. I started by asking him about one of the biggest criticisms of his books—that they teach people how to use steroids. As with cookbooks or home-improvement guides, just because you can read it doesn't mean you should be doing it. "Your book, *Building the Perfect Beast*, is a how-to manual for those who use steroids. What was your motivation for getting this information out?"

"I realize that some see it as such, but my intent was never to create a how-to guide," Rea responded. "My goal was to dispel many of the common beliefs regarding the use of anabolics and other substances. Though I do a great deal of consulting in the U.S. for the most effective longevity approaches to ethical hormone-replacement therapy, for many years now I have worked with athletes only while in Mexico or Thailand—for obvious reasons. Personally I feel that if you agree to compete under a specific set of rules or laws, it's only ethical and competitive if you do so."

Continuing with the idea that Rea's ideas are intended for a very certain market, I asked him to explain who his audience is. "Do most AAS users understand the types of things you teach in your book, such as proper cycles, how to differentiate between different protocols, and anabolic phases?"

"I would have to say that many do," he said. "But in truth there is a learning curve to deal with. There is so much of the old dogma and media/political mania clouding the realities. This is about science and health, not personal beliefs and preferences."

Given his openness toward AAS, it surprised me to find that he spends so much time in his books discussing supplements. "Many of the products listed in your book are available over the counter or at least over the net. How much of the gains you see your clients make are due to 'legal, nonbanned' products?"

"That would depend on where the athlete is located," Rea said carefully. "In regard to Thailand and South America, there is a preference toward anabolic steroids and other drugs. If we are talking about the U.S., I would have to say that most of the progress my own athletes enjoy is accomplished through legal over-the-counter means.

"Odd I suppose, to realize this, but in truth we really do have the ability to optimize the human body with supplements to produce very effectual levels of performance-oriented hormonal and related profiles. We certainly now have no problem optimizing natural testosterone product to a level that is as effective as moderate dosages of anabolic steroids. It would be legal and, even more important, health promoting."

Some of Rea's experience comes from building his own personal beast. In my research I found a web page that shows a dramatic change in his physique from 1982, when he weighed 127 pounds, to 1987, when he weighed 258 pounds (and not much looks like fat). I asked him, "Now, nearly twenty years later, you're nearly the same weight and looking like you're ready for a competition. Could you have made these gains, or held them, without the use of AAS?"

The now 263-pound Rea answered, "I have monitored well over a thousand chemically enhanced individuals, and it is not too difficult to see the errors many have made, or why. From blood-work returns and studies done with HRT patients, I have learned how to structure protocols for specific intent that do not compromise health.

"While living in Mexico I opted to push the envelope to prove what I have seen thousands of times: beasts can be built in a manner that does not destroy health and to a level that few realize is possible. I myself certainly had less than perfect genetics, but the results spoke for themselves. My point being that anabolic steroids and related substances played a pivotal role in the outcome."

In light of the conventional wisdom of steroids, his next answer surprised me. "As to maintaining the results without illegal AAS, the answer is yes to a very surprising degree. Anyone with the proper compounds at hand and the knowledge to apply them can realize results of a significant degree. I am not suggesting that supplementally we can compete with potential realized from no-rules-anything-goes criteria, but I am stating for a fact that we can match and exceed the results realized by so-called cheating athletes—without cheating. Of course you have to realize that monitored athletes have a far more limited array of items to use."

In essence, Rea is saying that the media's favorite spring training activity of the last few years is invalid. Simple eyeballing of a player's weight gain or loss of mass isn't likely to be a good indicator of his usage or nonusage of illegal substances. (As I write this, Ivan Rodriguez is being pilloried for coming to camp twenty-two pounds lighter. There hasn't been one story about his off-season work with Sari Mellman, a nutritionist who gets raves from her athlete clients usually reserved for cult leaders.)

Rea continued, "This is so and yet very WADA, IOC, and NFL friendly. We are on the edge of seeing maximum human potentiation that allows both enthusiasts and athletes alike to enjoy the results more common only to the few genetically gifted.

"The current trend is that we want all our athletes to perform like superhumans but to do so on cereal and vitamins. Yet we allow ourselves the freedom to maximize our own performance and aesthetics to a profound degree. Odd, huh?"

I noticed that Rea barely mentioned some of the substances that have been near faddish in some bodybuilding circles, the prohormones. "How effective are some of the new prohormones?"

"If you are referring to those that are now banned, some were very effective. Others just sucked."

"What about the new designer substances, like THG. Will they continue to find their way into sports?"

"Of course they will. It's human nature to improve on what has been done in the past. So there should be no surprise that many are not willing to accept the 'everyone is created equal . . . so act like it' scenario.

"In truth, what is the difference between this and someone who once used Viagra but replaced it with Cialis? Both are drugs that give an unfair advantage to the user. He is chemically enhanced to perform better than some who do not use them. By replacing the old 'couple hours of possibilities' realized from Viagra with thirty-six hours of 'how many times' with Cialis, they are only proving the point: humans love performance, will cheat to get it, and part of that is improving on what has been done in the past."

This was a very interesting point. "Why is there such a disconnect between sports performance and literal performance enhancers like Viagra/Cialis and the millions of other 'acceptable' prescription drugs available?"

"Simple!" Rea exclaimed. "The public and media alike give themselves allowances we do not give to our heroes and idols. The public can use erectile function and libido drugs, have plastic surgery to enhance breast and penile size, use liposuction to lose fat that a quality diet would remove and maintain. Then we tell our athletes to perform at superhuman levels without any means of superhuman recovery. How is that ethical? We live under a double standard and fail to accept it when others do not agree."

I wondered if Rea had put together something specific to baseball. "Are the types of programs you advocate good for specific sports, such as baseball? How would you go about training an athlete to be the perfect 'baseball beast'?"

"Geez, don't get me started!" he said with a laugh. "We have created a monster in the politics of sports, to a point that everyone— not necessarily the ones who know something—has a say. The result is that athletes do as many things wrong as they do right . . . and hope for a better contract next year."

He paused, thinking. "Blood work to see what the athlete has screwed up thus far, then some performance testing to look for errors in muscular acquisition and utilization. Much of this can be seen in old injuries not properly healed, which result in one muscle working against others, or the lack of synergy between the muscles employed. In short, reteaching the body to do its job correctly and efficiently by teaching the athlete to make every muscle play nicely with the others.

"Then a dietary evaluation that optimizes metabolic needs. And last, a look at hormonal levels and ratios to decide upon a specific supplementation, diet, and training program that best suits *that* athlete. By the way, we really are not all created equal," he said, laughing again.

That made sense, but I wondered if Rea's experience-based approach could give us the answers that the lack of research has left wanting. "The types of activities needed in baseball are very different from in any other sport. It's clear to see that an offensive lineman would want to be bigger and stronger, a sprinter would want to be more explosive. Where's the gain for a baseball player?"

"The ability to move any object through space requires factors of force and acceleration resulting in action and reaction," he explained. "In relation to physiological endeavors, this means the ability to produce muscular contractile force at a rate that is greater than the opposing force. Ever try to bat a ball with loose hands and a half-ass swing?

"In English this means that greater amounts of muscle—not just mere mass from fat that is inert weight, only good for acting as a barrier and force-absorption medium, like what is needed for a football lineman—potentially can generate greater mean mass contractile force. Put another way, more muscle and muscle mass results in the ability to exert greater force. The result is the ability to move the body through space at a greater rate and speed than less lean mass would allow, and the ability to hit or throw a ball harder, faster, and farther. Make sense so far?" The baseball guy inside me had a few quibbles with this, but I let him continue without interruption.

"Well, AAS also have some neural stimulation capacity. Some more than others. This means greater neurological stimulation and additional contractile activity. Those who have noted the increase in strength during ephedra use are experiencing the same idea." Of course ephedra is a banned substance in baseball, most closely connected to the death of Steve Bechler.

I wanted to stay with the baseball line, to discuss some of the seeming problems a "baseball man" would have: "There are no credible studies that show a stronger person will be a better hitter. Of course, there's a dearth of credible studies, period, in this field. In your experienced opinion, what do you think would actually be the advantage?"

He had a good analogy, explaining, "Most males have experience being in a fight once or twice in their lives. As a rule the larger man wins because he can hit harder with greater mean force due to greater muscle contractile capacity and weight. But if the larger man lacks the ability to hit a moving target, it means little— unless he can get hold of the smaller fellow. The same is true of any activity using speed and contractile force. Look at the truly great home run hitters. Though they got on base a lot in the earlier parts of their careers, it was not until they had increased lean mass tissue significantly that they had the power to hit the long ball."

Again, I'm not sure how much of this makes baseball sense, but it does follow with what Rea knows. I wasn't talking to him for his baseball expertise but for what he could teach me about performance enhancers. "Nonetheless it was their talent and hard work that made it happen. Size and contractile force make for a statistical advantage in all sports that don't require prolonged physical endurance."

Moving away from baseball, I got back into Rea's training programs. "You're famously selective about who you train, and I'll assume you wouldn't advocate illegal substances for a minor. Does it worry you that anyone can buy your book off the net and follow the programs?" I asked.

"First, I do not advocate illegal anything for anyone," he responded, quickly and emphatically. "I do not consult for use of AAS unless I am in Mexico with the client, or in the U.S. discussing possibilities with researchers or medically qualified individuals. Doing otherwise is not moral. It means you teach others, who trust you as an authority, to put themselves at risk. It's simply not acceptable.

"No, I am not really concerned in that regard. I feel strongly about ethics and love our industry. I offer a great deal of information in my books that gives those under twenty-one every reason not to use AAS and related compounds as they dramatically damage long-term potential. I also advocate not doing anything illegal. In truth, few readers under twenty-one can cope with the structural information in any of my writings."

Rea's books don't talk about building athletes, they talk about building dominant, powerful, record-breaking machines. He doesn't use the term "beast" for effect; he means it. "When you 'build a beast,' how much more can you make them?" I asked. "Toney Freeman came to you not to go, Atlas-style, from a ninety-eight-pound weakling to a monster, but from someone many people would say was unbelievably massive to . . . well, *more* massive. How much up from 100 percent can you take someone?"

"Percentages are not truly possible here due to so many variants. We are also talking about diet, focus, determination, pain thresholds, knowledge, and existing genetics. How one trains and diets makes a huge difference in any athlete's potential, regardless of sport," he said.

"I will say this, if ethics and health issues were not a large, controlling factor in my life, I would say, potentially, that anyone with all the variants in line could realize a 75 to 100 percent increase above that possible through so-called natural training and supplementation." Yes, I was stunned by this statement. "Of course, this is in relation to actual lean muscle mass, not necessarily performance. In this scenario, performance could actually suffer dramatically. As to performance enhancement, 15 to 30 percent is not a stretch of reality at all—if all training and dietary factors are in line." This is an interesting concept. A 100 percent gain might realistically cause a relatively small gain in performance or an actual reduction. It made me think of Jason Giambi's numbers in 2003 and 2004.

I wondered where Rea felt AAS belonged in sport. "Do you believe that AAS should be illegal or banned?"

His answer was simple. "Legal, medically supervised by competent personnel, and age dependent." There's not much to question there.

While Rea certainly knew his material, I wondered if he actually believed, like many do, that use of AAS could be healthy. "You seem to think that chemistry is as important as genetics or work ethic when it comes to muscle building and retention. Can an athlete actually be healthier on your program than he would be without the use of these substances?"

I hit a passion point with this question. Rea responded, "I wrote the books because of this. I certainly did not do so for the money. Being a book author is basically minimum wage. I was simply sick of the lies.

"There is so much dogma that puts potential AAS users at risk. My goal has been to help others realize the risks of poor judgment and improper information. I intentionally cite the hundreds of studies used to compile the information. Of course I also use personal experience to help readers relate. In short, I strongly support legal healthy choices based upon facts, not mere supposition."

"What's the next step—genetics, more advanced steroids, something else?"

"There will always be those who focus on beating a governing method such as IOC and WADA. For them it will likely be the alteration of genetics by way of material manipulation and the use of growth-regulating factors like Mechano-Growth Factor and members of the growth factor superfamilies," he responded. "There will always be new so-called designer steroids as well. But the governing bodies really are getting much better at playing that game, so those initiatives will be progressively limited. The sad thing is that some of the structures really have merit for hormone-replacement therapy and longevity uses as well as sexual dysfunction. Others are just evil substances.

"For those who opt to play by the rules, the new goal should be super-overcompensation of natural metabolic pathways. [Rea's concept of going so far above and beyond nature was breeding superlatives the size of his athletes.] As an example of one endogenous anabolic pathway, we actually can make the body naturally produce two to five times its normal testosterone levels while reducing estrogen production and improving cardiovascular health. More lean tissue through improved recovery and immune function results in a superior potential for athletic performance. Better, healthier athletes certainly should not offend anyone."

Rea touched briefly on the more "accepted" use—and I use that term cautiously—of AAS, testosterone, and other substances for anti-aging functions. The baby boomers will do almost anything to stay young, rivaling athletes in their willingness to experiment. "Will a greater acceptance of steroid-like substances in anti-aging therapies make them more acceptable for bodybuilding and other sports?"

"It already has to a small degree, but there are a few clinics fueling the wrong fire due to improper prescribing practices. I have consulted for several, and at times I find myself in a position where I need to terminate our contract and refer them to a good criminal attorney if they choose to continue doing business as is," he said ominously. That's not a good sign. "With the media and political-fueled hysteria and pro athletes writing books based upon obvious lies, there is a strong move toward zero tolerance and very high expectations for these clinics. In the long run I do think the realities of beneficial hormone replacement therapy will prevail."

I wanted to let Rea end on the note that brought me to him. I wanted to give him a chance to clear up what he felt was misunderstood about his field. "As a leading educator on this topic, what do you find is the greatest misconception the general, uneducated public has about AAS?"

He sighed. "Where to start? That steroids kill people and are somehow evil is probably the worst. I have known thousands who have used insane dosages of AAS for fifteen to twenty years, and they have fewer side effects than if they took Tylenol!

"Consider the number of women who have used oral contraceptives for decades. These are oral steroids, boys and girls, and they are alkylated—altered in a manner that increases liver toxicity just like some oral AAS. Just because it is a female sex hormone does not mean it is nice. They are more toxic than most nonalkylated injectable AAS. Yet women live in spite of their steroid— uh, birth-control use.

"Please do not misunderstand: only an idiot would tell you that any drug is totally safe, and AAS certainly are drugs. The problem is the lack of proper supervision and the laws that have made medical personnel inept at knowing anything of value about the subject."

Many experts may not agree with Rea, but he certainly makes a credible case for what he believes. Spending time with Rea and with Rick Collins further opened my mind to the possibilities and issues surrounding performance-enhancing substances, such as AAS. It will surprise many that the men who advocate the use of these drugs support strict controls, medical supervision, and age limits as well as the right of sports sanctioning bodies to ban certain substances.

Listening to the arguments and facts of Rea and Collins made me realize that the discussion to this point hasn't been one-sided—it's been no-sided. Instead of facts and honest, substantive debates, we tend to fall back on emotion. Once again, there's a new shade of grey about this issue that we should all be aware of.

14

Do Steroids Rewrite
the Record Books?

THERE'S NO DOUBT that steroids have had an impact on the game of baseball, but determining the extent of their statistical repercussions is a thorny issue. Have steroids pumped up the numbers? At first glance the obvious answer is a resounding "Yes!" The BALCO transcripts have cast the accomplishments of players like Barry Bonds in a new and less flattering light, tainting records no less hallowed than the single-season and all-time home run marks.

The admissions of Jason Giambi, as well as public declarations by Ken Caminiti and Jose Canseco, have placed the accomplishments of several Most Valuable Players in a dubious realm as well. Meanwhile the routine crossing of statistical plateaus once reserved for the Cooperstown-worthy elite by muscle-bound sluggers—and those not so muscle-bound—has placed a further shroud of guilt on numerous players.

On the other hand, the extent of the influx of performance enhancers over the last decade or two is difficult to track. So far as we know, and even with Canseco's admissions, no Patient Zero exists from whose vantage we can say with complete confidence, "All records past this point are suspect." We lack any credible evidence that would indicate how widespread the use of performance-enhancing drugs was at a given time. This vague epidemic of steroid users has infiltrated the game at a time of accelerated change, as expansion, realignment, interleague play, and a host of new ballparks have altered the playing field both literally and figuratively. Discerning the impacts of those factors is difficult enough. Add adjustments to the strike zone, changing tastes in baseball bats, and the widespread and oft-refuted charge that the baseball itself has been tampered with and you have an issue so murky that it's no wonder so many theories abound.

The basic argument for the impact of steroids on the game starts with the parallel rise of home runs and overall run scoring over the past couple of decades. In order to understand those increases, it's necessary to look much further into baseball history. Is it truly reasonable to call this time in baseball's storied history the "Tainted Era"?

A graph of historical scoring since 1900 shows similar trends in both leagues over time, with seemingly random spikes here and there. Viewing by decade smoothes out the rough spots, but the trends can be emphasized or deemphasized depending upon where one chooses to draw the lines. For the purposes of this chapter, we're going to take years ending in "3" as the start of the decade. This accomplishes a couple of things: it neatly separates the designated-hitter era (which began in 1973) from the decade before it, and it catches the recent trend of increased homers and run scoring at the point where those rates began to climb steadily upward. We'll simply tack on 2003 and 2004 to the 1993–2002 decade, and 1901 (when the American League began play) and 1902 to the 1903–1912 decade. Here, then, is the historical breakdown of run scoring by "decade":

RUNS PER GAME

	National League	American League
1901–1912	4.02	4.02
1913–1922	3.95	4.13
1923–1932	4.84	5.02
1933–1942	4.40	5.07
1943–1952	4.34	4.33
1953–1962	4.45	4.39
1963–1972	3.97	3.87
1973–1982	4.11	4.33
1983–1992	4.09	4.47
1993–2004	4.67	5.02

We can see that the current "Tainted Era" isn't even the highest scoring, whether or not the pundits who complain of football-like scores care to admit that. The 1923–1932 National League and 1933–1942 American League eras were both higher scoring. By a more conventional definition of decades, the twenties rank as the NL's highest-scoring period (4.72 runs per game) and the thirties as the AL's most prolific (5.25 runs per game).

It's worth noting that a list of the top ten seasons for scoring in either league since 1901 includes only a few seasons after World War II:

National		American	
1930	5.68	1936	5.67
1929	5.36	1930	5.41
1925	5.06	1996	5.39
1922	5.00	1938	5.37
1999	5.00	1901	5.35
2000	5.00	2000	5.30

National		American	
1923	4.85	1932	5.23
1903	4.78	1937	5.23
1953	4.75	1994	5.23
1935	4.71	1939	5.21

But while the current levels of scoring have some precedent, the same can't be said of home run rates. Keeping in mind that we're looking at home runs per team per game, here's a chart following the same decade breakdown as above:

HOME RUNS PER GAME

	National League	American League
1901–1912	0.15	0.13
1913–1922	0.24	0.20
1923–1932	0.49	0.43
1933–1942	0.49	0.60
1943–1952	0.63	0.55
1953–1962	0.94	0.84
1963–1972	0.75	0.81
1973–1982	0.68	0.79
1983–1992	0.74	0.89
1993–2004	1.03	1.11

The recent rise in home runs isn't just the result of a fluke season here or there; it's a sustained change. Here is how the increase has proceeded over the past two decades, again in home runs per game:

	National League	American League
1985	0.73	0.96
1986	0.79	1.01
1987	0.94	1.16

	National League	*American League*
1988	0.66	0.84
1989	0.70	0.76
1990	0.78	0.79
1991	0.74	0.86
1992	0.65	0.78
1993	0.86	0.91
1994	0.95	1.11
1995	0.95	1.07
1996	0.98	1.21
1997	0.95	1.09
1998	0.99	1.10
1999	1.12	1.16
2000	1.16	1.19
2001	1.14	1.11
2002	1.00	1.09
2003	1.05	1.10
2004	1.10	1.15

The top ten seasons for homers per game in each league are mostly from the 1993–2004 period:

National		*American*	
2000	1.16	1996	1.21
2001	1.14	2000	1.19
1999	1.12	1999	1.16
2004	1.10	1987	1.16
2003	1.05	2004	1.15
1955	1.03	1994	1.11
2002	1.00	2001	1.11
1998	0.99	1998	1.10
1956	0.98	2003	1.10
1996	0.98	1997	1.09

Further evidence of this power surge can be found in considering the number of players reaching various plateaus in a single season. To account for expansion, we can express this as the number of twenty-, thirty-, or forty-homer hitters per team:

PLAYERS PER TEAM HITTING X HR

	20 HR	*30 HR*	*40 HR*
1901–1912	0.01	0.00	0.00
1913–1922	0.09	0.03	0.02
1923–1932	0.61	0.30	0.11
1933–1942	0.91	0.34	0.08
1943–1952	0.96	0.31	0.06
1953–1962	1.97	0.65	0.27
1963–1972	1.74	0.55	0.13
1973–1982	1.52	0.35	0.06
1983–1992	1.88	0.48	0.06
1993–2004	2.63	1.07	0.34

Clearly, any way you slice it, home runs are up. Are steroids to blame for this power surge? It's certainly possible that they are contributing to the increases in home runs. Yet, as mentioned before, this surge has taken place against a backdrop of accelerated change in baseball, and it's worth exploring some of those changes for clues as to their impact.

EXPANSION

From 1901 through 1960, the major leagues consisted of sixteen teams, eight in each league. Before the 1961 season, two American League franchises were added, and two National League teams followed the next year. Two more teams were added to each league for 1969, and a pair of teams was added to the AL for 1977. But after adding ten teams over a sixteen-year span, the leagues stayed the same size until the NL added a pair in 1993. The next expansion took place in 1998, with one team being added in each league and one team switching from the American to the National League. The most prevalent complaint about these successive waves of expansion is that there just isn't enough competent pitching to support more teams, that each new expansion team spreads the equivalent of another ten or so AAA-caliber pitchers around the majors. If one considers the broader talent base the majors have to draw from nowadays, this argument becomes dubious.

In 1960 the United States Census counted more than 179 million people. The 2000 Census counted more than 281 million, an increase of about 57 percent. In the same period the number of major league teams grew from 16 to 30, an increase of 87.5 percent. That pace has outstripped the growth of the U.S. population, true enough. But in 1960 only 9.6 percent of major league players were born outside the United States. A 2003 report by the Commissioner of Baseball showed that 27.8 percent of players on Opening Day rosters were born outside the United States. The addition of Latin America—particularly Venezuela (24 million), the Dominican Republic (just under 9 million), and Puerto Rico (4 million), which combined to produce 18.6 percent of those 2003 Opening Day rosters—to the talent base, as well as a growing number of players from the Pacific Rim, has easily compensated for the expansion of teams.

This of course makes no mention of the pre–Jackie Robinson issue of racial segregation in baseball. Before that historic change in 1947, baseball in effect self-limited its talent pool. Knowing that the Negro League had players like Josh Gibson, with all the power of a Babe Ruth, it's possible that the numbers from this era are skewed downward by the use of what, in a more equitable game, may have been players that could not have made the major leagues.

Nonetheless it's not very difficult to check the numbers to see what kind of effect expansion is having on home runs. A quick look at the eight waves of expansion shows that, lo and behold, per-game home runs have increased in all but one expansion season:

EXPANSION AND HOME RUNS

American	Pre	Post	Additions
1960–1961	0.88	0.95	Los Angeles Angels, Washington Senators II
1968–1969	0.68	0.85	Kansas City Royals, Seattle Pilots
1976–1977	0.58	0.89	Toronto Blue Jays, Seattle Mariners
1997–1998	1.09	1.10	Tampa Bay Devil Rays
AL Total	0.82	0.95	

National	Pre	Post	Additions
1961–1962	0.97	0.89	New York Mets, Houston Colt .45s
1968–1969	0.55	0.76	Montreal Expos, San Diego Padres
1992–1993	0.65	0.86	Colorado Rockies, Florida Marlins
1997–1998	0.95	0.99	Arizona Diamondbacks (+ Milwaukee Brewers to NL)
NL Total	0.78	0.88	
ML Total	0.80	0.92	

Altogether, expansion years have seen home runs increase by 14.5 percent. But before we go pointing the finger at the dilution of pitching talent as the cause for these increases, a few caveats come with the data.

First off, any student of baseball history can point to the inclusion of 1968–1969 data as a bit sketchy. The so-called "Year of the Pitcher," 1968, saw run scoring in both leagues reach lows that hadn't been seen in years; in fact 1968 represents the AL's all-time low, and the lowest the NL had seen since 1908. Major rule changes, including the lowering of the mound and the redefinition of the strike zone, went into effect in 1969, restoring scoring to more familiar levels. Home run rates weren't as drastically suppressed in 1968, but the NL hadn't seen as low a rate since 1946, while the AL hadn't been so low since 1954. But since both leagues had seasons approaching those low home run rates within the next several years, the 1968 data can't really be considered an anomaly.

The 1977 expansion coincided with a shift in the supplier of baseballs. Through 1976 Spalding had manufactured the balls, but Rawlings took over as the sole provider the following year. Although no change in the manufacturing process was announced, the power spike was undeniable. Home run rates jumped 53.4 percent in the AL and 46.5 percent in the NL, which contained the same twelve teams and ballparks as the year before. The role of changing baseballs in this power explosion will be explored further below.

The 1993 expansion introduced Major League Baseball to high altitude in the form of the Colorado Rockies. Playing in the accurately named Mile High Stadium (home of the Denver Broncos), the Rockies and their opponents hit 184 homers in the thin air, an average of 1.14 per game. In all other NL games, homers were hit at a rate of 0.81 per game. The Rockies and their opponents, now playing in Coors Field since 1995, have continued to outpace the league's home run rate by a considerable margin.

It's tempting to claim that expansion can account for at least some of the increase in home runs. But with the exception of the 1993 expansion, homers have fallen back to previous levels within a year or two after introducing the new teams, suggesting that the "expansion effect" is either the result of randomness or merely short-lived. As for that anomaly, the Rockies' role raises the question of how much impact the ballpark, rather than the quality of pitching, has to do with this power surge. So to the parks we turn.

BALLPARKS

The past fifteen years have constituted a building boom for Major League Baseball. It will no doubt be a major part of the legacy of Commissioner Bud Selig. Expansion added four new parks while no fewer than fourteen of the twenty-six previously existing teams switched to new venues between 1991 and 2004. The boom hasn't ended, either. The Montreal Expos' transfer to Washington, D.C., means that another new ballpark (beyond the stopgap RFK Stadium) will enter the game in short order. The Cardinals have a new stadium scheduled to open in 2006, and teams like the Florida Marlins, Oakland A's, and Minnesota Twins may strike the right mix of owner cooperation, corporate sponsorship, and public largesse to build new parks by the end of the decade. Like the steroid issue, this unprecedented turnover makes a convenient culprit for the coinciding rise in home runs. How much water does this theory hold?

The trend away from larger, multi-purpose ballparks (such as Cleveland's Municipal Stadium, which held 78,000) toward more intimate ones (Jacobs Field in Cleveland holds 43,368) has carried the perception of new bandboxes where baseballs easily leave the yard. But the average distances of the outfield fences are very close to what they were fifteen years ago, before the spate of new stadiums:

THE CHANGING BALLPARK, FENCE DISTANCES

NL	LF	LCF	CF	RCF	RF
1990	331.3	375.8	402.6	375.8	331.0
2004	333.0	375.5	404.5	379.6	332.5
change	+1.8	−0.3	+1.9	+3.8	+1.5

AL	LF	LCF	CF	RCF	RF
1990	327.1	378.1	406.1	374.9	323.1
2004	328.7	377.9	403.3	374.6	324.4
change	+1.6	−0.1	−2.9	−0.3	+1.3

In the National League, fences are actually farther away than they were before. In an effort to compensate for the high altitude, Coors Field's center field is 415 feet deep. Houston's Minute Maid Stadium, which is near sea level, is even more immense with a 435-foot center field that attempts to compensate for an archaically short left-field foul line (315 feet) but creates problems of its own with the amount of ground outfielders must cover. Yet those two parks are the league's most conducive to run scoring and home runs.

In the American League, foul lines are a bit longer than they were 15 years ago, but center field is a few feet closer. Even the 420-foot center field of the Detroit Tigers' Comerica Park is 20 feet closer to home plate than in the old Tiger Stadium. Shorter foul lines at the White Sox's U.S. Cellular Field than at old Comiskey Park have made that park one of the more homer-conducive, but then Oriole Park at Camden Yards, which replaced Memorial Stadium's 309-foot foul lines (the shortest in the majors during this period) with a 333-foot left-field line and a 318-foot right-field line, is another homer haven. Changes in the fence distances themselves don't do a very good job of explaining the rise in home runs.

The impact of a park on the amount of home runs hit there is often expressed as a number near 100, which itself is defined as the league average. A home run park factor (HRPF) of 110 means that a park elevates home runs by 10 percent above the league average, while a park factor of 90 means that it decreases home runs by 10 percent. Because the year-to-year variations can contain a bit of noise due to random influences such as weather and injuries to key players, analysts often use three years' worth of data to create park factors.

The park factors for 2004—which are based on 2002–2004 data except for the parks that have opened even more recently—show that many of the new parks are at extremes for either promoting or preventing home runs. Of the top ten homer havens, six of them were built during this recent boom and one other,

Toronto's Skydome (recently rechristened the Rogers Centre; note that for purposes of clarity we will generally refer to ballparks by the building's original name) arrived in 1989, just before the boom. Only two of the parks in the 1990 top ten are in the current one, and only four of those old parks are still open:

TOP TEN PARK HR FACTORS

2004 Park, Team	*HRPF*	*Opened*
Coors Field, COL	134	1993
Comiskey II, CHW	131	1991
Bpk at Arlington, TEX	120	1994
Olympic Stadium, MON	118	1977
Wrigley Field, CHC	117	1916
Great American, CIN	116	2003
Citizens Bank, PHI	113	2004
Dodger Stadium, LAD	113	1962
Bank One, ARI	113	1998
Skydome, TOR	112	1989

1990 Park, Team	*HRPF*	*2004 HRPF*
Riverfront, CIN	130	—
Skydome, TOR	127	112
Wrigley Field, CHC	125	117
Jack Murphy, SDP	125	—
Anaheim Stadium, ANA	123	88
Tiger Stadium, DET	120	—
Kingdome, SEA	120	—
Arlington Stadium, TEX	120	—
Veterans Stadium, PHI	111	—
Fenway Park, BOS	108	90

The other side of the coin is very similar: six of the bottom ten parks are new, and only two parks make both lists. But six of the 1990 bottom ten were still open in 2004, though Olympic Stadium, which placed in the top ten in 2004, is now closed.

BOTTOM TEN PARK HR FACTORS

2004 Park, Team	HRPF	Opened
Petco Field, SDP	71	2004
Pac Bell, SFG	77	2000
Pro Player Stadium, FLA	82	1993
Comerica Park, DET	82	2000
Jacobs Field, CLE	84	1994
Busch Stadium, STL	85	1966
Shea Stadium, NYM	87	1964
Anaheim Stadium, ANA	88	1966
Metrodome, MIN	88	1982
Tropicana Field, TBD	89	1998

1990 Park, Team	HRPF	2004 HRPF
Royals Stadium, KCR	64	105
Astrodome, HOU	67	—
Comiskey Park, CHW	75	—
Busch Stadium, STL	82	85
Oakland Coliseum, OAK	85	110
Municipal Stadium, CLE	89	—
Dodger Stadium, LAD	89	113
Three Rivers, PIT	92	—
Shea Stadium, NYM	94	87
Olympic Stadium, MON	95	118

Of course, with six new parks in the top ten and six new parks in the bottom ten, that leaves the other six new parks in the middle ten— a distribution we'd expect given eighteen new parks out of thirty.

Ultimately it's tough to discern trends via this approach because park factors are relative rather than absolute, and they've been in constant flux for the past fifteen years. But one way to look at the issue is to examine the park home run factors of the ballparks that were in place *before* the boom that started in 1991. There are twelve parks in this group:

Home Team	*Park*
Anaheim Angels	Anaheim Stadium (now Angel Stadium)
Boston Red Sox	Fenway Park
Chicago Cubs	Wrigley Field
Los Angeles Dodgers	Dodger Stadium
Minnesota Twins	Metrodome
Montreal Expos	Olympic Stadium
New York Mets	Shea Stadium
New York Yankees	Yankee Stadium
Oakland A's	Oakland-Alameda County Coliseum (now McAfee Coliseum)
St. Louis Cardinals	Busch Stadium
Toronto Blue Jays	Skydome (now Rogers Centre)

Because the Expos played twenty-two home games in Puerto Rico in each of the past two years, sending their park factors into complete disarray (their single-year park HR factor was 89 last year, 146 the year before), it's probably best to remove them from this group. We already know that the remaining parks are distributed somewhat evenly between the top, middle, and bottom tens, but it's worth tracking how their aggregate park HR factor—using single-year data rather than three-year data, because otherwise we're triple-counting these years in our averages—has changed over time. Alongside those numbers are a list of the new ballparks introduced into the league, and their average park HR factors since opening:

TRACKING THE OLD PARKS

	HRPF	New Parks
1990	104.5	
1991	104.4	Comiskey II (107.2)
1992	95.5	Camden Yards (108.5)
1993	101.7	Pro Player (88.0), Mile High (111.8)
1994	101.7	Jacobs Field (98.4), Ballpark in Arlington (107.0)
1995	99.4	Coors Field (149.3)
1996	100.8	
1997	103.3	Turner Field (97.3)
1998	98.9	Bank One (107.3), Tropicana Field (99.4)
1999	99.3	Safeco Field (91.6)*
2000	101.5	Enron Field (112.0), Pac Bell (76.4), Comerica (75.6)
2001	101.2	Miller Park (109.0), PNC (88.4)
2002	103.8	
2003	100.2	Great American (115.5)
2004	100.8	Petco (71.3), Citizens Bank (113.1)

*does not include split season between Kingdome and Safeco in 1999

Before the boom started, these eleven parks combined to be a bit above average with regard to home runs. While the park factors have bounced around a bit over the years, they're still a few hairs above average, though in recent years that effect has leveled off. Overall they're at a 101.1 HRPF. All of this suggests that newer, more homer-conducive parks have pushed the average slightly upward.

Again it's worth remarking upon how many of the new ballparks are at the extremes. Of the nineteen new venues introduced above (including Mile High and Coors Field as two parks), only three have been within 5 percent of the league averages since inception. Five of them are at least 10 percent over the league average (though two of those are extremely new), and five are at least 10 percent under (one of them is extremely new).

It's tempting to say that much of the hype linking inflated home run totals to the new ballparks is focused on the extremely conducive ones while ignoring the fact that an equal number of those parks dampen home runs. We hear about Coors Field all the time, but how often does Comerica Park come up? Also, it should be pointed out that Barry Bonds's feats have taken place in a park that's extremely unfavorable for home runs, possible ammunition for those drawing a link between his admitted PED use and his amazing performance.

INTERLEAGUE PLAY

After much discussion, debate, and handwringing on the part of purists, interleague play finally began in 1997. While some of the games, particularly the intrastate "natural rivalries" between teams like the Yankees and Mets or Cubs and White Sox, draw a fair amount of attention, the reality is that these games have grown fairly banal over the years. In part that's because, in the end, not only do inevitable pairings like the Pirates versus the Twins fail to stimulate significantly more interest or draw more fans, but their 5-4 games more or less resemble any other 5-4 games on the docket.

Interleague play, which has made up about 10 percent of the overall major league schedule over the past eight seasons, has had no significant effect on either scoring or home runs. The scoring average is right where it should be—the same number of runs (4.84) has been scored per game in interleague play as in non-interleague play. As far as home runs are concerned, they're slightly higher in interleague play:

HOME RUN RATES FOR INTERLEAGUE PLAY

	AL	NL	Int	Non-Int
1997	1.09	0.95	1.05	1.02
1998	1.10	0.99	1.04	1.04
1999	1.16	1.12	1.15	1.14
2000	1.19	1.16	1.21	1.17
2001	1.11	1.14	1.16	1.12
2002	1.09	1.00	1.00	1.05
2003	1.10	1.05	1.14	1.06
2004	1.15	1.10	1.09	1.13
Total	1.12	1.06	1.11	1.09

The difference between homers in interleague and non-interleague play is a mere 1.5 percent, an increase that's hardly overwhelming—about eight homers per year. If interleague play is having an effect on home runs, it's either extremely minor or simply a random artifact of a smaller sample size.

RULES

From the realm of the quantifiable (if not crystal clear), we move to factors that are less easily measurable. One is changing rules, namely the redefined strike zone. Over the years the zone has been tinkered with as a means of maintaining the delicate balance between pitchers and hitters, and that tinkering has occurred with increasing frequency since expansion began.

Back in 1887 a strike was defined by the rulebook of the time as a pitch that passes over home plate "not lower than the batsman's knee, nor higher than his shoulders." Additional definitions of strikes caused by foul balls and foul tips were added within a few years, but that basic definition of the strike zone wasn't touched until 1950, when it became the space over home plate "between the batter's armpits and the top of his knees when he assumes his natural stance."

In 1963 the zone was expanded to include the top of the shoulders, but after several lean years for scoring, climaxed by 1968, it was redefined for the 1969 season as between the batter's armpits and the top of his knees. From this point to the start of the power boom, the strike zone progressively shrunk in practice. Strikes above the waist were seldom called, while some umpires began calling pitches just outside the plate as strikes. Greg Maddux, perhaps the best pitcher of this era, described the strike zone in 1994 as "about the size and shape of a paperback book."

Fast-forward to the 1987 season, which saw spikes in home runs and scoring that are more in line with the 1993–2004 era than they are with their own surrounding decade. That year home runs rose 19.5 percent in the NL and 15 percent in the AL. Most notable, perhaps, was the forty-nine-homer season turned in by Oakland A's rookie first baseman Mark McGwire. Even singles hitters like Wade Boggs and Tony Gwynn reached career highs in home runs that season. Perhaps as a direct reaction to the barrage of homers, the strike zone was redefined in 1988, with "the upper limit of which is a horizontal line at the midpoint between the top of the shoulders and the top of the uniform pants." (This in fact appears to be narrower than the preceding zone—but umpires were calling it narrower still.)

The changes didn't end there. In 1996, after the new offensive boom was well under way, the lower end of the zone was moved to the bottom of the knees, but still the high scores continued. Finally in 2001, Major League Baseball decided that the umpires were taking too much liberty with their individual interpretations of the strike zone, which tended to be shorter (not calling the high strike) and wider (too generous with pitches a couple of inches off the plate) than the rulebook definition.

Baseball decreed a more rigid interpretation of the strike zone and introduced the QuesTec Umpire Information System, a network of computers and cameras used to independently evaluate each umpire's pitch-calling accuracy. The system has been marked by controversy, with umpires and pitchers registering the bulk of the complaints. Most famously, Curt Schilling smashed a QuesTec camera in 2003.

In the expansion era, the first few changes in strike zone definitions coincided with home run rates shifting in the intended direction—that is, an expanded zone should be expected to favor pitchers and thus decrease home runs:

THE CHANGING STRIKE ZONE'S EFFECTS ON HR RATES

NL/AL	HR/G	Zone	Net
1962N	0.89	increase	
1963N	0.75		−0.14
1962A	0.96	increase	
1963A	0.92		−0.04
1968N	0.55	decrease	
1969N	0.76		+0.21
1968A	0.68	decrease	
1969A	0.85		+0.17
1987N	0.94	increase	
1988N	0.66		−0.31
1987A	1.16	increase	
1988A	0.84		−0.32
1995N	0.95	increase	
1996N	0.98		+0.03
1995A	1.07	increase	
1996A	1.21		+0.14

NL/AL	HR/G	Zone	Net
2000N	1.16	enforce	
2001N	1.14		−0.02
2000A	1.19	enforce	
2001A	1.11		−0.08

The 1996 change, which should have favored pitchers, appears to be an exception, as does the 2001 enforcement, which by taking away the tough pitches just outside the plate and leaving the more hittable ones directly over it, should have favored hitters. If we add it all up carefully, scoring the intended effects as positive and the unintended ones as negative, we get an impact of 0.08 HR/G, meaning that the average zone change moved the home run rate 0.08 HR/G in the direction intended by the change.

In magnitude, that's about two-thirds of what we observed for the expansion effect, though in this case the intent has generally been toward decreasing homers. More important, since the years within the 1993–2004 period have not been affected as intended, it's increasingly difficult to attribute the recent rise in home runs to any change in the strike zone.

EQUIPMENT

So it is that we come to the next major possibility and the one most shrouded in secrecy, the baseball itself. Perhaps more than any other culprit, "juiced baseballs" could certainly explain the rise in home runs. Unfortunately, much of the evidence for changes in the ball is anecdotal and cloaked in perennial denials from manufacturers and other officials. Still, a stroll through the annals is enlightening.

Recall that when Rawlings took over from Spalding as the supplier of major league balls in 1977, it coincided with a 50 percent jump in homers across the two leagues. It's not that 1977 rates were unprecedented; both leagues had been at similar heights as recently as 1970, itself a spike year for homers. That year Cubs manager Leo Durocher had observed, "The ball not only seemed smaller and lighter than the 1969 ball, but the pitchers tell me that the stitching was tighter and the seams weren't as raised as the other ball." The fact is that the 1976 home run rates per game (0.58 in the AL, 0.57 in the NL) were abnormally low; the AL hadn't seen such a big homer drought since 1948 while the NL hadn't been so low since 1968.

Before the switch in manufacturer, the last major change to the ball had been in 1974, when the outer coating switched from horsehide to cowhide because of a shortage of the former. Homer production fell from 0.80 per game in each league to 0.64 in the NL and 0.70 in the AL. It continued to slide toward 1976 levels in the NL but rebounded to 0.76 in the AL the next year before its 1976 dip.

Taking all that into consideration, we're left with only speculation. Perhaps Spalding didn't perfect the process of using the new covering before surrendering the manufacturing process to Rawlings. Perhaps the balls used at the end of their run were leftovers that were slightly substandard in resilience, leading to the dip in home runs. It would take a "Deep Throat" type of source to provide insight into the matter, but unlike the Watergate scandal of that decade, none has ever come forward. In any event, aside from 1976 the rises and falls around that time fit right in with the garden-variety, season-to-season variation in the expansion era.

It's worth reviewing the composition and construction process of major league balls here. The ball starts as a pill of cushion cork (a mixture of cork and ground rubber) wrapped in two layers of rubber, one red and one black. The pill must weigh 0.85 (+/- 0.05) ounces and measure 1.375 (+/- 0.01) inches, and is polished to remove the rubber seams from the molding process. The sphere is then tightly wrapped with three layers (166 yards) of wool yarn and one layer (150 yards) of cotton/polyester yarn. After each layer, the balls are measured to ensure they fall within specifications for size (+/– ⅟₁₆ inch tolerance), weight (+/– ⅟₁₆ ounce tolerance), and tension.

Once wound, the ball is trimmed of excess tailings, coated with a layer of latex adhesive, and then surrounded by the familiar two pieces of leather, which are hand-sewn together with 88 inches and 108 stitches worth of waxed red thread. The balls are then machine-rolled for about 18 seconds to compress the seams, dried in a dehumidifier, and rolled again before being cosmetically graded to check for abrasions and blemishes. They are then measured and weighed again. In the final analysis, balls must measure 9 to 9.25 inches in circumference across two seams, 2.86 to 2.94 inches in diameter, and weigh from 5 to 5.25 ounces. From there they are stamped, weighed, inspected again, and hand-packed for shipping.

After they arrive at a central warehouse, approximately 28 of every 10,000 balls are run through tests. The balls are shot out of a pitching machine at 85 miles per hour into a white ash board. The ball's speed coming off the board is measured to determine its co-efficient of restitution. Balls must rebound at between 43.69 and 49.13 miles per hour to meet standards.

Note that at every stage, some amount of tolerance is allowed. That tolerance translates onto the playing field—or rather off it. According to a 2000 study at the University of Massachusetts–Lowell Baseball Research Center (funded by Major League Baseball and Rawlings), "two baseballs could meet MLB specifications for construction but one ball could be theoretically hit 49.1 feet further." It is often said that baseball is a game of inches, but here we have evidence direct from Major League Baseball that it can be a game of feet. Take that whopping difference into account and it's not difficult to imagine how the slightest differences in the balls from year to year could lead to a plethora of towering 425-foot home runs instead of lazy 375-foot fly balls.

The winding of the ball is the most shrouded in secrecy of any manufacturing stage. Once upon a time, balls were hand-wound. At some point, winding machines came into use. A June 5, 2000, *Sporting News* article about the manufacturing process, written by Stan McNeal, noted that the winding room was off-limits to photographers because of Rawlings' desire to keep its machines secret from the competition. Wrote McNeal of what goes on inside:

> The inspections during the winding process are so precise it would be too difficult to juice the ball at this step. After each layer of yarn is wound on the ball, it is weighed and measured. Within the target weight, there is a variance of .04 ounces—which is what, the weight of a strand of hair? If the ball doesn't fit inside the variance, it is kicked back.
>
> Now if Major League Baseball wanted to change the specs and juice a ball, it could do it in the winding room. With the balls wrapped a little tighter, they would become a little harder and fly off the bat a little farther.

Speculation about changes in the ball's manufacturing process abounds virtually every time home runs are on the rise. The result is waves of intrepid sportswriters doing in-depth pieces that produce familiar tropes from players, coaches, and executives. Take 1993, when home runs rose 32.7 percent in the NL (hello, Rockies) and 16.8 percent in the AL.

Writing in *Sports Illustrated* that year, Tim Kurkjian drew this quote from Cardinals pitching coach Joe Coleman: "The ball is livelier—or else the ozone layer is messed up again. . . . I've compared balls from last year and this year, and this year's are noticeably harder. Our pitchers never got blisters last year, but this year a bunch of them have. The seams last year were soft; this year they're hard. With the seams being higher on the ball, it creates more air-time—it keeps spinning and carrying." Note that Coleman blamed higher seams for the rise in homers while Durocher, twenty-three years earlier, blamed lower seams.

Coleman's claim drew a denial from Scott Smith, marketing services manager for Rawlings. "The baseball has not changed in any way," Smith told Kurkjian. "There has been no change in material or in the manufacturing process. It is the most consistent baseball ever made." Smith surfaces often in the litany of ball-juicing literature. In 1994, with homers still rising before the players' strike—up 10.7 percent in the NL and 21.7 percent in the AL—Smith told Robert Sanford of the *St. Louis Post-Dispatch*, "None of the manufacturing processes nor any materials have been changed. The major leagues have not changed specifications. Therefore, the balls have not changed."

But a report the same year by *Newsday's* Mark Herrmann drew information from an employee at the Rawlings plant in Costa Rica, where the ball has been manufactured since 1988 (the first balls from that plant were used in the 1989 World Series):

> "Now that you mention it, they did change things six months ago," [employee Manrique] Solano told David Scanlan, a Canadian journalist based in Costa Rica. "They used to give us the insides [of the ball] stuffed in the leather cover. All we had to do was sew it together. Now we have to put the insides into the leather ourselves, then sew it."
>
> In terms of leading to answers on the home run question, that went about as far as a bunt single. Scanlan later said, in a telephone interview, that he wasn't allowed to see the assembly line inside the wooden building, which looks like a school.

Fast-forward to 1996, when home runs were on their way to rising another 12.9 percent in the AL (they were virtually unchanged in the NL). The *Post-Dispatch's* Jeff Gordon asked Smith about conspiracy theories on changing construction of the ball.

"That would probably take a committee vote of the owners," Smith said. "There would be a review of the rules committee, and there would have to be a testing period, probably in spring training."

If baseball managed to keep the change quiet, Smith said, "Then they would have to expect thousands of employees at our plants wouldn't tell somebody that they were doing something different. There are just too many people."

That same year Smith told Bob Klapisch of the *Bergen Record* that such a conspiracy "would make for a secret bigger than Watergate."

The ball came under intense scrutiny during the 2000 season, after a spate of early home runs prompted articles like the *Sporting News* piece already noted. This time Major League Baseball decided to do something about it, funding the testing at UMass-Lowell. Led by Professor Jim Sherwood, a team of mechanical engineers put 192 vintage balls from 1999 and 2000 through a litany of tests and accompanied Major League Baseball personnel on tours of the plants where various components were manufactured, issuing a 28-page report on its findings.

The tests "revealed no significant performance differences and verified that the baseballs used in Major League games meet performance specifications." Yet the engineers also found that "some of the internal components of the dissected samples were slightly out of tolerance on baseballs from each year. These out-of-tolerances are despite the thorough inspection process in place at the assembly plant in Costa Rica." And 13 of the 192 baseballs supplied (6.8 percent) were underweight. It was this team that came up with the 49-foot flight discrepancy between baseballs that were within tolerance specifications. The research team also noted that minor league balls, with pure cork centers (as opposed to cushion cork, which contains ground rubber), didn't fly quite as far, a shortfall of about eight feet. This is an interesting illustration of how minor changes in the core manifest themselves.

The tests didn't satisfy everybody. That year several independent researchers also tested 2,000 balls against older stock, but those tests are of questionable validity since the older balls had not been stored in a climate-controlled environment. A test sponsored by the *Cleveland Plain Dealer* that year, which didn't involve using aged baseballs, drew some interesting results. Engineers at the Lansmont Corporation in Silicon Valley were asked to replicate National Bureau of Standards liveliness tests on baseballs that had been done almost sixty years earlier and found that the major league balls sampled could fly up to forty-eight feet farther than their 1942 counterparts.

Of course, anecdotes abounded that year as well. An article in *Popular Mechanics* written by the former major league pitcher and Yankee broadcaster Jim Kaat reported no shortage of pitchers observing inconsistencies in balls:

> Juiced or not, and MLB's position notwithstanding, pitchers, umpires, and coaches—folks who handle the ball every day—say there is a difference. Everyone we spoke to says that the cover is slick. Mike Reilly, who has been an umpire for more than 20 years, thinks so. Before every game, umpires rub up five dozen brand-new balls with a specific mud from the Delaware River to take the shine off. He said that the mud doesn't adhere to the new ball the way it did to the old ball.
>
> Cal Eldred, veteran pitcher with the Chicago White Sox, says, "You used to get a baseball, gather a little perspiration off your brow or off your wrist, rub the ball maybe twice in your palms and you got the feeling you wanted. Now, I go to my wrists and I rub the ball 10 or 12 times and my hands just keep slipping off it."
>
> . . . New York Yankees pitchers David Cone and Andy Pettitte told me that the [newer] ball is not only smoother, but that

the stitches are inconsistent. Some are wide, others thin. They say that most of the time, the stitches are flatter than they used to be. . . . Pettitte insists that when he played inter-league ball in previous seasons, he could feel a big difference in the National League balls—he said that they had higher seams.

Baseball can say all it wants about the components of the ball being the same. Every major-league clubhouse I go into provides an opportunity to talk to players who handle the ball, and they all tell me the same thing: There's a slickness to the ball that wasn't there before.

Kaat pointed out that Major League Baseball began stamping its big blue logo on the ball in 2000, making its spin easier to track—and thus revealing its break—on its way to the hitter. The UMass report conceded that was one avenue left untested.

Speaking of hitters, it's worth at least an aside to remark on the potential impact of new bats. Once upon a time the big sluggers swung the biggest sticks. Babe Ruth swung war clubs as heavy as fifty-six ounces and reportedly favored a forty-seven-ounce model during his sixty-homer season in 1927. Teammate Lou Gehrig wielded a thirty-eight-ounce bat. Al Simmons used a forty-six-ounce stick while Rogers Hornsby went as high as fifty ounces. Today such weights would be unthinkable, and sluggers such as Barry Bonds and Ken Griffey, Jr. use bats weighing as little as thirty-two ounces.

What's more, those bats have different properties than their predecessors. Hillerich and Bradsby's Louisville Sluggers, which are made of ash, still hold about 60 percent of the major league market, but as of 2002 no fewer than forty-eight manufacturers were supplying bats. Bonds and many other major leaguers have switched to maple "Sam Bats" made by the Original Maple Bat Company of Ottawa. Maple is slightly denser than ash but much more durable, allowing for thinner barrels and hence lighter and faster-swinging bats while maintaining the size of the bat's sweet spot.

Such lighter bats help batters generate more speed and more control while allowing them to wait a fraction of a second longer—choosing a more desirable pitch—before deciding whether to swing. But a lighter bat doesn't translate into hitting the ball farther, corked-bat controversies to the contrary. As Robert K. Adair, the author of the definitive *Physics of Baseball* wrote:

> From elementary principles of mechanics, we can say with complete reliability that for a given bat speed, a heavy bat will drive a ball farther than a light bat. Conversely, for a given kinetic energy of the bat, a light bat will drive the ball farther than a heavy bat (for bat weights greater than 20 ounces). To this we add the (very plausible) condition that no player can swing a heavy bat faster than he could a light bat. And we hold that no player can put more energy into a light bat than into a heavy bat. The energy transmitted to the bat is simply the product (better, integral) of the force of the bat that the hands apply along the direction of motion times the distance through which the hands move. If we assume that the arc of the hands—and bat—is the same for a light or heavy bat, the larger force that it is possible to apply to the more slowly moving heavy bat will result in a larger energy transfer to that bat.

Adair employs several theoretical models in his section on bat properties, and each time comes to the same conclusion: with everything else constant, heavier bats drive the ball farther. But for some players, the additional reaction time allowed by swinging a lighter bat may well outweigh the slight gain in distance produced by adding a few ounces.

BECAUSE OF THEIR outlaw status, steroids make a convenient culprit for the latest power surge in baseball. Their illegality and the dangers they may pose to users provide a convenient outlet for moral outrage. The fact that many of the leading sluggers of the day have been implicated, either by their own testimony or the more dubious allegations made by others, suggests that there may be something to this.

But baseball over the past decade and a half has seen no end of changes that may account for the rise in home runs often attributed to steroids. Expansion and newer (though not necessarily smaller) ballparks may be contributing factors, though neither completely explains the rise. Developments in equipment—both under-the-radar changes in balls and more publicized developments in bats—may well be driving it.

If so, that should come as no surprise, as changes in equipment have had a huge impact on the quality and style of play over major league history. Just think of the impact of the cushion cork ball in the 1920s, or improved gloves. Most notably, scientific tests done on Major League Baseball's dime even show that balls on one edge or another of official tolerances may be contributing to this boom, with minute and unreported changes in components along the complex chain (say, the yarn or the rubber) making one year's batch "hotter" than another.

Ultimately, blaming the rise in homers on scantily documented changes in the ball brings us back to a similar spot that blaming the rise on steroids does—namely, the realm of speculation and uncertainty. It's likely we'll never know what changes in the baseball were made over the past two decades any more than we'll know how many players were juicing in that time.

That's not the easiest answer to swallow, even with an educated guess here and there. It will be worth watching to see whether the enforcement of Major League Baseball's new drug-testing policy coincides with a decline in home runs. Perhaps taking the juice out of the players will take the juice out of the statistics—or perhaps this era isn't so tainted after all.

15

What Lies Ahead

TRYING TO PREDICT what the next generation of performance-enhancing drugs will be is a little like gazing into a crystal
ball and hoping that images do not appear. It would be hopeful
but naive to think that with all the drug education and drug testing now in place, the use of performance-enhancing drugs will
diminish. If we look at the history of PEDs and the motivational
factors involved with their use, we can see that barrier inhibi-
tions have broken down and that the problem will be with us for
a long time.

The three greatest motivations are desire to excel, desire for
glory, and money—not necessarily in that order. I have met very
few athletes or other physically active individuals who did not
wish to perform better. Regardless of how much they practice,
condition, lift, or watch their diet, they will reach a plateau beyond which they may or may not be able to achieve better results.
Some extremely hardworking individuals may outperform or over-
achieve their physiological limitations. Others, for various reasons,
may not reach their potential. But the vast majority are not content to remain at their current level.

There are also societal expectations for performance. Not long ago, interest in Major League Baseball seemed to be diminishing after an unpopular strike and fan resentment of inflated salaries. Then, along came the Sosa-McGwire home run race of 1998. Everyone was either watching baseball, reading the sports pages, or watching sports reports to see which player had hit home runs that day. They were also going to the ballpark and buying Major League Baseball apparel in record numbers. The fans were back in a big way, because this is what they wanted to see for their baseball entertainment dollar. If fans went to a game and no home runs were hit, they were disappointed.

The desire for glory is exemplified in a survey that asked young athletes if they would take a drug that would guarantee them an Olympic gold medal or national championship, even if they knew the substance would cause them to die within five years. Astonishingly, more than 90 percent of those polled said they would take the substance.

Money as a motivating factor in the use of performance-enhancing drugs can be seen in Major League Baseball, where the minimum salary is $320,000 per year. Sammy Sosa's fine of one day's salary for skipping the last game of the 2004 season was $87,000. And professional athletes can, because of their status, make a lot of money endorsing products. Many baseball players did not have opportunities for higher education or the acquisition of marketable skills; if they weren't playing professional baseball their standard of living and everything that goes with it would be far out of their reach.

A major concern of many athletes is therefore to find better ways to take performance-enhancing substances and not get caught. Remember that drug tests are not as omnipotent as the general public is led to believe. Unless there is an established test for the substance, it will not be found by testing. That's why so many athletes who were using THG passed their drug tests—there was no established test for THG until a sample of the substance was sent to the World Anti-Doping Agency by a disgruntled coach. The scientists were then able to do some "reverse engineering" and develop the test that eventually led to suspensions of track and field athletes in 2004. For anabolic steroids, drug tests still depend on distinguishing between naturally occurring testosterone and testosterone from extrinsic sources.

Sports federations are constantly racing to stay ahead of performance-enhancing drug use, though critics of the anti-doping effort claim that the money being spent on developing new testing technologies is not nearly enough to make a serious effort at curbing drug use among athletes. There is also much governmental lip service to stopping the use of performance-enhancing drugs that is not backed up by action.

One voice that has been unusually quiet on the issue of drugs in sports is the Office of National Drug Control Policy, headed by John Walters. Unlike his predecessor, General Barry McCaffrey, Walters has taken a passive position. He has not held a single national news conference on sports drug policy and has sent well-meaning but lesser surrogates (his deputy director and general counsel) to international conferences instead of personally appearing.

Under Walters and the George W. Bush administration, the United States has been delinquent with dues to the World Anti-Doping Agency—inexcusably and severely hampering the organization's ability to test and conduct research. And when the WADA and the International Olympic Committee, with eighty nations represented, announced the creation of the world code for drug testing, Walters merely put out an all-but-ignored statement. In terms of real action, the post-McCaffrey White House drug czar's office has done next to nothing. It even refused to host a summit on drugs and sports when USA Track and Field begged it to do so after the THG discovery—asserting that the White House Drug Office does not respond to "press statements."

It should be the responsibility, even the job description, of the drug czar to publicly and actively educate athletes and the public. He should be a high-profile advocate. It is hypocritical for some pro athletes to be exempt from the accepted world standard for fair athletic competition. Without real, visible support beyond political posturing from the drug czar and the White House, groups such as the World Anti-Doping Agency and the International Olympic Committee will have reduced leverage against athletes and players who oppose serious drug testing. Perhaps we should return to amateur representation in the Olympics instead of sending the "dream teams" of professionals whose unions oppose the type of testing imposed on other participating athletes.

With the exception of biogenetic engineering, which we have already explored, what we are likely to see in the future of performance-enhancing substances is more of the same, with improvements in their effects and better ways of masking them so that they will not appear on a drug test.

Secretogues are substances that, when ingested, cause greater stimulation of the secretion of another substance, such as testosterone. Secretogues are currently on the market as dietary supplements which claim to enhance the secretion of testosterone and human growth hormone by the body. We need more research to determine the efficacy of these substances today, but in the future it is highly possible that secretogues may be one of the optimal avenues to avoid positive drug tests.

When a substance occurs naturally in the body and is secreted by the body, it would seem virtually impossible for current drug-testing technologies to detect the substance (testosterone, HGH) as exogenous (a source from outside the body). Benchmarking is the only possible detection technique, and it's not foolproof.

Sport supplements will play an even larger role in chemical performance enhancement in the future. Due to constraints on regulation, substances can be developed and marketed without going through the three-phase program required for prescription drugs. As long as the product contains a dietary substance, it passes muster as a legitimate supplement. It is highly likely that, through further research, these products will become more sophisticated in providing performance-enhancing capabilities.

Developers of designer steroids can be counted on to produce substances that are custom-fitted, stealth-like, and undetectable. They already have drugs for which no credible test has yet been developed, such as human growth hormone, probably the most commonly used banned substance by elite athletes today.

It is well known that there are synthetic anabolic steroid formulas (the reported numbers range from seventeen to fifty-seven) that were never produced before anabolic steroids came under legal scrutiny. It would not be difficult for a chemist to use these formulas. Since these designer steroids were not "in physical existence" at the time the anabolic steroid control acts were passed, they are not a controlled substance. And because they were never previously produced, there would be no existing drug test to detect them.

Masking agents, though they now exist, will become an even more important part of the performance-enhancing drug scene in the future. Masking agents will inhibit the excretion of waste materials that indicate anabolic steroid use. The past few years have seen a refining of chemicals that can mask the use of steroids. Many of them are sufficiently effective that laboratory staff testing urine can easily be misled, especially if the use of a new masking agent produces confusing results.

Epitestosterone (which is almost impossible to distinguish from naturally occurring testosterone), dextran (plasma extender), diuretics, finasteride, and probenecid are masking agents that have been used somewhat successfully in the past. The most effective masking agents are still to come. Smart but unethical chemists will find them and will find a waiting market for them among athletes seeking the "edge."

Dr. Patrick Schamasch of the World Anti-Doping Agency worries about genetic enhancements. "Injections of synthetic EPO and human growth hormone will be nothing by comparison. If somebody increases the production of hormones by direct genetic manipulation—what are you going to do?" He adds, wearily: "And we're always a little bit behind."

16

How to Save the Game

THERE IS NO moral to this story.

Having learned what I learned in the writing of this book, I can only hope that the denouement of this story is a better discussion of the issues. I believe that education, not enforcement, is the best path to a solution of baseball's drug problems.

The historic agreement between Major League Baseball and the Players' Association in the 2004–2005 off-season is a good start. Both sides saw that something had to be done. Was it enough? That remains to be seen. It's certainly a big step forward and an improvement over the conditions of 2002 or even 2004. It won't be perfect and likely never will. A drug-testing program is, at its heart, more about public relations than it is about cleaning up a sport.

In writing this book I've avoided an agenda. I came in neither pro-steroid nor anti-steroid in the most general sense while still opposing the use of steroids in the game of baseball. I have no "dog in this hunt," as some might say.

In the end, I'm left wondering about the motives of those other than the players in this drama. Do they truly want performance-enhancing drugs banned for aesthetic reasons, or do they believe that PEDs have assaulted the integrity of the game? Do they hope to make millions of dollars, either as a creator or a distributor of these drugs? Is their objection simply an expedient political stance?

What we need most is scientific research. We know too little about steroids and other performance-enhancing drugs to make intelligent, reasoned decisions about a proper course of action. It is difficult, but not impossible, to do research that will give us more knowledge about what works, what doesn't, and how to react to new substances or even get ahead of the curve.

As with drug use, we'll probably never know the true motives of most people associated with the issue of steroids. I do know that all of us, from the Commissioner of Baseball down to the fan in Section 552, can do better. We each have a unique obligation to educate ourselves and others in an attempt to make baseball the best game possible.

It's important to reiterate that there are no easy answers to be found. Any complex issue with a major emotional component will require a precipitating event before there can be a breakthrough. I've become convinced that this is for the best. In the absence of easy answers, we must continue thinking and talking, which will keep us from making hasty judgments.

If this is indeed a "Tainted Era," writers and analysts a generation from now will be able to add the necessary historical context. The question for those of us in the here and now is, what can we do today?

In basements, on ballfields, and even in the major leagues, research—theoretical and practical—is ongoing. Organizations like BALCO are certainly not alone in doing research and using athletes as their subjects. People who ordinarily have no motive besides making money are peddling PEDs like any other street drug. In the best-case scenario, athletes get an anabolic steroid;

worse, it may be nothing more than water or something toxic cooked up in an underground lab.

Baseball has taken steps to curb drug usage but has done little to combat the causes of such usage. I'm not sure it wouldn't be more effective to educate than to test. It will take a wholesale change in the win-at-all-costs mentality that permeates baseball today, and that can only begin at the grassroots. The simple joy of the game escapes us from time to time. The deleterious effects of some of these drugs, especially those typically used outside of therapeutic settings, must be widely publicized. It's clearly not enough to say that the use of PEDs is cheating; that hasn't worked so far, and it's not likely to be suddenly effective.

This is a problem not only of money but of will. Baseball—both the players and Major League Baseball itself, personified by the commissioner—must begin a program of education, research, and public relations. In 2004 baseball put only $100,000 into research. While that figure was tripled for the 2005 season, it remains less than the value of one first-year player. This clearly shows where baseball's values lie.

The game deserves better, but the situation may not be as bleak as most of us imagine. A former player told me he thinks there are fewer drugs in baseball now than when he played, even with steroids. But if we agree that steroids have no place in the game, one is too many.

The historic accord on testing between the owners and the players must be allowed to play out. Evidence must be collected, assessed, and, if necessary, punishment meted out fairly. Moreover, with this program in place, those who have called for such testing must be willing to accept its results and consequences. Wild West justice and trial by public opinion must end.

We've had too many bystanders in recent years. It's no secret that the Lords of Baseball have profited immensely from what has been called the "Steroid Era." I don't believe they have done much more than sit idly by. They haven't been organized about anything else in the last fifty years, so I won't grant them this vast conspiracy. It doesn't let them off the hook, either, for doing nothing about this problem for far too long.

Reporters haven't done their jobs in the locker rooms. Reaching in to grab a bottle of andro isn't investigative journalism, but it's better than the "Shocked! Shocked!" cries from the beat writers who knew what was happening. Somewhere along the line, beat writers grew lazy—not all, but far too many. They're happy getting their quote from the media-savvy player or manager rather than telling us something new. Their reward will be replacement unless they change. We're already seeing this.

The players did what they thought was necessary, though no one thought enough of the game itself to step up. Jose Canseco's tell-all is ten years too late. Ken Caminiti spoke only after his career ended. We understand the why of the users, yet no one explains the complicity of the silent majority.

Finally, fans too deserve their share of the blame. We followed along, suspending disbelief as our heroes shattered records and led our teams to victory. People don't like to question their heroes, and without evidence it's only speculation. But there was no outcry for a real testing policy until well after it could have been instituted. Fans flocked to games in record numbers, following the home runs as they flew out of ballparks, and generally accepted a game that for some appeared to be "out of whack." They fueled the fire with their combustible dollars trailing behind them.

This book has forced me to take a hard look at aspects of the game I've taken for granted at best and willfully ignored at worst. I hope that learning the facts, understanding the people, hearing the motives, and seeing the possibilities will lead you to the same place. It's a hopeful place, where the ultimate goal is making the game of baseball not only better but safer.

A Note on the
Authors and the Text

WILL CARROLL, primary author of *The Juice*, is the most authoritative analyst of medical issues in baseball. His column, "Under the Knife," appears regularly in Baseball Prospectus and is, according to Hall of Famer Peter Gammons, "essential reading." Mr. Carroll also hosts a weekly syndicated radio show. His first book, *Saving the Pitcher*, about the prevention of pitching injuries in modern baseball, has become a standard for doctors, athletic trainers, and pitching coaches. He lives in Indianapolis.

WILLIAM L. CARROLL, ED.D., wrote chapter 3, on the history of performance-enhancing drugs; chapter 4, on the effects of steroids; chapter 5, on amphetamines and uppers; chapter 6, on supplements; and chapter 15, on the next generation of drugs. Dr. Carroll is professor of Human Performance and Exercise Science and director of the Athletic Training Education Program at the University of Mobile in Alabama. He has more than thirty years' experience as an athletic trainer and college educator, has worked with college, professional, and international teams, and has taught internationally. He serves as an examiner and accreditation site visitor for the National Athletic Trainers Association. He is a state-licensed and nationally certified athletic trainer.

This book has relied heavily on the contributions of four experts in their fields, who have helped bring a rounded perspective to this book that would not otherwise have been possible:

JAY JAFFE contributed chapter 14, on the supposed effects of performance-enhancing drugs on the baseball record books. Mr. Jaffe is the founder of Futilityinfielder.com and an author of Baseball Prospectus, and has cultivated a passion for statistics since the day he discovered that fractions were merely batting averages in disguise. He is a graduate of Brown University and works as a graphic designer in New York City.

KEITH SCHERER contributed chapter 9, on legal issues. A native of Chicago, he is a trial attorney with extensive experience as both prosecutor and defense counsel. He has been an author of Baseball Prospectus and is a leading sabermetrics writer.

KYLE SERIKAWA contributed chapter 11, on performance enhancement via genetics. He works as a laboratory manager for a facility at the University of Washington that helps researchers apply genomic technologies to answer biological questions. He is also a freelance science writer. He received his Ph.D. in genetics from the University of California at Berkeley and currently works and writes in Seattle.

MICHAEL DAVID SMITH contributed chapter 8, on steroids in the National Football League. He writes for FootballOutsiders.com and has a special interest in line play and the history of football. He is a graduate of the University of Illinois and lives in Chicago with his wife, Sarah.

A Note on the Authors and the Text

The authors wish to thank the team of experts at Baseball Prospectus, Pat Arter, Gary Huckabay, Keith Law, Thomas Gorman, Dave Haller, Blake Kirkman, Chaim Bloom, Peter Gammons, Steve Fainaru-Wada, Howard Bryant, Alex Belth, Richard Askren, Michael Overdorf, Millard Baker, Pat Cotter, Doug Rawald, Dr. Ron Lee, Andra Hardt Jaffe, Becky Drees, Brandon Chizum, Greg Rakestraw, Brad Wochamurka, Scott McCauley, Craig Rath, Christian Ruzich and All-Baseball, Ken Arneson and his crew, and Aaron Schatz and the Football Outsiders, Zachary D. Manprin, Aegis Sciences Corporation, and our families.

Index

Index

Index

Index

Index

Index